Hessen
Landesabitur 2013
Abitur-Training
Englisch

Autorinnen und Autoren:
Manuela Becker, Eva-Maria Bienek, David Clarke, Petra Hobrecht, Kerstin Köhler, Maren Köhn, Susanne Mikus-Binkowski, Martin Weinreich

Manuela Becker stellte die Inhalte für diesen Band zusammen.

Der Abdruck der Trainingsaufgaben erfolgt mit freundlicher Genehmigung der Kultusministerien in Bayern, Hessen, Nordrhein-Westfalen und des Sekretariats der Ständigen Konferenz der Kultusminister der Länder in der Bundesrepublik Deutschland (KMK).

HESSEN LANDESABITUR 2013

Abitur-Training

ENGLISCH

Trainingsaufgaben mit Lösungen

Cornelsen

Die in diesem Werk angegebenen Internetadressen haben wir überprüft (Redaktionsschluss: Juli 2012). Dennoch können wir nicht ausschließen, dass unter einer solchen Adresse inzwischen ein ganz anderer Inhalt angeboten wird.

Herausgeber: Bibliographisches Institut GmbH, Mannheim
Marketing & Vertrieb: Cornelsen Schulverlage Marketing GmbH, Berlin

Das Wort **Cornelsen** ist für die Cornelsen Verlag GmbH als Marke geschützt.

Alle Rechte vorbehalten.
Das Werk und seine Teile sind urheberrechtlich geschützt. Jede Nutzung in anderen als den gesetzlich zugelassenen Fällen bedarf deshalb der vorherigen schriftlichen Einwilligung des Verlags. Weder das Werk noch seine Teile dürfen ohne Einwilligung eingescannt und in ein Netzwerk eingestellt oder sonst öffentlich zugänglich gemacht werden. Dies gilt auch für Intranets von Schulen und sonstigen Bildungseinrichtungen.

© 2012 Bibliographisches Institut GmbH
Dudenstraße 6, 68167 Mannheim
2., aktualisierte und überarbeitete Auflage
Projektleitung: Anja Sokoll/Marion Clausen, Berlin
Redaktion: Regina Sidabras, Berlin
Gesamt- und Umschlaggestaltung: Torsten Lemme, Berlin
Layout und Herstellung: cs print consulting, Berlin
Druck und Bindearbeiten: orthdruk, Bialystok, Polen
Printed in Poland
ISBN 978-3-06-150152-5

Gedruckt auf säurefreiem Papier,
umweltschonend hergestellt aus chlorfrei gebleichten Faserstoffen.

Vorwort

So trainieren Sie für die Abiturprüfung 9

Hinweise zu den Prüfungsbestimmungen

Wie läuft die Prüfung ab? 10
Wie lange dauert die Prüfung und welche Hilfsmittel sind erlaubt? 10
Wie ist die Prüfung aufgebaut? 11
Welche Themen werden geprüft? 11
Was sind Operatoren und Anforderungsbereiche? 13
Wie gehe ich am besten an die Aufgaben heran und worauf sollte ich beim Bearbeiten achten? 14
Wie wird die Arbeit bewertet und wie viel zählt sie für die Endnote? 15
Kann man sich noch mündlich prüfen lassen? 15

The Challenge of Individualism

USA: The American Dream
Trainingsaufgabe 1: Comprehension, analysis, comment or re-creation of text (Sachtext) (GK und LK*) 18
Thomas L Friedman: The New 'Sputnik' Challenges: They all run on oil

Living together (illegal immigration: Hispanics)
Trainingsaufgabe 2: Summary, comparison and letter to the editor (comment) (Sachtext) (LK) 26
Embracing Illegals

Science and Technology

Ecology
Trainingsaufgabe 3: Summary, rhetorical analysis, making a speech (Sachtext) (GK) 32
Naomi Klein: You can't eat public relations

Them and us

The one-track mind (prejudice, intolerance, ideologies)
Trainingsaufgabe 4: Comprehension, interpretation and comparison, discussion (Sachtext und Cartoon) (LK) 40
Suzanne Goldenberg: Religious rights fights science for the heart of America
Patrick Hardin: What's it all about?

---

* GK = Grundkurs, LK = Leistungskurs

Tradition and Change

The United Kingdom: Social change

Trainingsaufgabe 5: Comprehension, analysis, evaluation (Sachtext) (LK*) . 46
Tony Blair's Lord Mayor's Banquet Speech

Work and Industrialisation

Industry and environment

Trainingsaufgabe 6: Comprehension, analysis, evaluation (Sachtext) (GK) .. 54
Cynthia Tucker: US Excess Vs. Nature's Limits

Extreme situations

The troubled mind

Trainingsaufgabe 7: Description, analysis, discussion (Romanauszug) (LK) .. 64
Stephen Amidon: Human Capital

The Dynamics of Change

Promised lands: Canada

Trainingsaufgabe 8: Comprehension, interpretation, discussion (Romanauszug und Sachtext) (GK und LK) 72
Margaret Atwood: Oryx and Crake
Margaret Atwood: Survival

Political issues

Trainingsaufgabe 9: Summary, comparison, discussion (Sachtext) (GK und LK) 80
Margaret Davis: New Beginnings

Order, vision and change

Models of futures: utopias, dystopias, progress in the natural sciences

Trainingsaufgabe 10: Summary, interpretation, discussion (Sachtext) (GK) . 88
New technology too advanced for own good

* GK = Grundkurs, LK = Leistungskurs

Ideals and reality

Structural problems (violence, (in-)equality)

Trainingsaufgabe 11: Summary, characterisation, comparison, discussion (Kurzgeschichte) (LK*) 94
Joyce Carol Oates: Love, Forever

Mediation

Multiculturalism

Trainingsaufgabe 12: Mediation (Sachtext) (LK) 102
Armin Laschet: Von den Zuwanderern lernen

Trainingsaufgabe 13: Mediation (Sachtext) (GK* und LK) 108
Nicola Jacobi: Weit weg von Zuhause – Minderjährige Flüchtlinge in Deutschland

Anhang

Formulierungshilfen und Redewendungen 114

Originalprüfung 2012 Grundkurs

Prüfung 126
Lösung 133

---

* GK = Grundkurs, LK = Leistungskurs

So trainieren Sie für die Abiturprüfung

Dieser Band ermöglicht Ihnen eine gezielte Abiturvorbereitung: Im Mittelpunkt steht das Training anhand von Aufgabenstellungen, die genau zu den Anforderungen Ihres Abiturjahrgangs passen.

Das Kapitel „**Hinweise zu den Prüfungsbestimmungen**" informiert Sie über alle wichtigen Bestimmungen und den Ablauf der Abiturprüfung. Besonders hilfreich ist das Verzeichnis der **Operatoren** (Handlungsanweisungen), in dem Sie die Formulierungen der Aufgabenstellungen erläutert finden (s. S. 13 f.).

Im Hauptteil finden Sie Aufgabenstellungen und Materialien, mit denen Sie sich konkret auf Ihre Abiturprüfung vorbereiten können. Die Aufgaben wurden sorgfältig ausgewählt; dabei wurden die wichtigsten Aufgabentypen, die geforderten Themengebiete und die nützlichsten Lösungsstrategien berücksichtigt.

Zu jeder **Trainingsaufgabe** finden Sie vorab eine Tabelle mit Angaben über
- den Aufgabentyp,
- das Thema,
- das zugrunde liegende Material,
- die Textsorte,
- das Niveau (Grundkurs und/oder Leistungskurs).

Hinweise geben zusätzliche Hilfen zum Verständnis und zur Bearbeitung einzelner Aufgaben.

Die **Lösungsschritte** zeigen, wie Sie in einer sinnvollen Reihenfolge den Weg zur richtigen Lösung planen und umsetzen können.

In der **Stichpunktlösung** sind die wichtigsten Lösungsaspekte zusammengestellt. Vergleichen Sie Ihre eigene Lösung mit der Stichpunktlösung und analysieren Sie auf dieser Basis Ihre Stärken und Schwächen.

Zu einigen Aufgaben werden Ihnen **ausführliche Lösungen** angeboten, die Ihnen als Beispiel für Ihren eigenen ausformulierten Text dienen sollen.

Auf vielfachen Wunsch der Nutzer bieten wir im **Anhang** eine Übersicht mit Formulierungshilfen und Redewendungen zum Nachschlagen.

Am Ende des Bandes finden Sie die **Originalprüfung** aus dem Jahr 2012. So haben Sie die Möglichkeit, eine reale Prüfungssituation zu simulieren.

Bei der Vorbereitung auf das Abitur und für die Abiturprüfung selbst wünschen wir Ihnen viel Erfolg!

Hinweise zu den Prüfungsbestimmungen

Wie läuft die Prüfung ab?

Seit 2007 werden in Hessen zentrale Abituraufgaben gestellt. Das erfüllt manche Prüflinge im Vorfeld mit Nervosität, denn anders als bei einer Kursarbeit können Sie nicht versuchen, Ihrem Lehrer/Ihrer Lehrerin möglichst genaue Informationen zur Vorbereitung zu entlocken. Allerdings hat sich gezeigt, dass es keinen Anlass zur Furcht gibt, denn Sie können am Tag der Prüfung aus drei Vorschlägen auswählen, d. h., Sie haben ein breites Spektrum an möglichen Texten und Themen zur Auswahl. Trotzdem müssen Sie sich genau auf alle Kursthemen vorbereiten. Hierzu ist es sinnvoll, sich die genaue Schwerpunktsetzung der einzelnen Halbjahre nochmals vor Augen zu führen und Ihr Material diesbezüglich zu sichten.

Die Durchführung der Prüfungen ist an den hessischen Schulen unterschiedlich geregelt. Während an den meisten Schulen die Arbeiten unter Aufsicht des Kurslehrers im Kursraum geschrieben werden, wird es an kleineren Schulen so sein, dass alle Schülerinnen und Schüler des Jahrgangs in der Aula die Abiturklausur gemeinsam schreiben.

Zu Beginn der Prüfung stellt die Aufsichtsperson die Frage nach Ihrer Gesundheit. Wenn Sie sich gesund fühlen und die Prüfung beginnen, müssen Sie sie auch zu Ende führen, und die Prüfung wird in jedem Fall gewertet. Wenn Sie sich krankmelden, können Sie den Nachschreibetermin wahrnehmen. Sie müssen innerhalb von drei Tagen ein Attest einreichen.

Natürlich ist es erlaubt, während der Prüfung kurz zur Toilette zu gehen, aber Sie dürfen in der Abwesenheitszeit keinen Kontakt zu anderen Personen aufnehmen (oder zur Cafeteria gehen). Allerdings müssen Sie sich bei der Aufsicht abmelden (d. h., Sie werden in eine Liste eingetragen) und auch wieder zurückmelden. Es wird jeweils nur eine Person aus dem Prüfungsraum entlassen.

Am Ende der Prüfung müssen Sie alle Unterlagen, auch Ihr Konzeptpapier und Ihre Gliederung, abgeben.

Die schriftlichen Prüfungen finden unmittelbar vor den Osterferien statt. In der Regel beginnen die Prüfungen um 9 Uhr. Die genauen Prüfungstermine werden Ihnen von der Schule zu Beginn des Schuljahres bekannt gegeben und Sie können diese auch auf der Internetseite des Kultusministeriums einsehen. Hier finden Sie weitere wichtige Hinweise, die zum Teil auch im Laufe des Prüfungsjahres noch aktualisiert werden. Es lohnt sich also, sich dort genau zu informieren: www.kultusministerium.hessen.de (dort finden Sie die Links *Schule – Gymnasium – Landesabitur*). Auf der Internetseite finden Sie auch Hinweise zur Durchführung und Bewertung sowie eine Musteraufgabe.

Wie lange dauert die Prüfung und welche Hilfsmittel sind erlaubt?

Die Prüfung im Grundkurs dauert 180 Minuten, im Leistungskurs 240 Minuten. Vorher haben Sie 45 Minuten Einlesezeit. In dieser Zeit können Sie die drei Vorschläge sichten und einen Vorschlag auswählen. Wenn Sie sich für einen Vorschlag entschieden haben, können Sie Ihre Wahl nicht rückgängig machen. Prüfen Sie also die Vorschläge genau und machen Sie sich eventuell schon jetzt eine Stichpunktsammlung, um zu prüfen, ob Sie alle Fragen ausführlich genug beantworten können. Am Ende der Einlesezeit werden die nicht ausgewählten Vorschläge eingesammelt und die Aufsicht vermerkt Ihre Entscheidung im Prüfungsprotokoll.

Neben einem einsprachigen Wörterbuch stehen Ihnen auch Wörterbücher Deutsch-Englisch zur Verfügung, damit Sie die Mediationsaufgabe besser bewältigen können. Allerdings sind alle elektronischen Geräte (besonders Handys) sowie elektronische Übersetzungshilfen **nicht erlaubt**.

Es ist sinnvoll, eine Armbanduhr mitzunehmen, damit Sie Ihre Zeit für die Bearbeitung einteilen können. Ein Handy kann auch zu diesem Zweck nicht benutzt werden.

Außerdem können Sie im Prüfungsraum die offizielle Operatorenliste (Bearbeitungsanweisungen) einsehen. Die offiziellen Operatoren werden auch in diesem Heft benutzt, und Sie sollten sich schon bei der Vorbereitung genau die unterschiedlichen Operatoren einprägen und die damit verbundenen Anforderungen einüben.

Wie ist die Prüfung aufgebaut?

Es werden Ihnen drei Prüfungsvorschläge zur Auswahl gestellt, die im Prinzip ähnlich aufgebaut sind. Im Grundkurs umfasst die Textlänge 500–700 Wörter, im Leistungskurs 700–900 Wörter, in der Regel mit drei Aufgaben, die den jeweiligen Anforderungsbereichen zugeordnet sind. Einem der Vorschläge ist eine Mediationsaufgabe vorangestellt, d. h., dieser Prüfungsvorschlag beginnt mit einem deutschen Text, der in Englisch zusammengefasst werden muss. Dafür ist der englische Text in der daran angeschlossenen Textaufgabe etwas kürzer als bei den anderen beiden Vorschlägen. Die Bewertung erfolgt 1:3 (d. h., die Mediationsaufgabe wird einfach gewertet, die verkürzte Textaufgabe dreifach).

Welche Themen werden geprüft?

Im Abitur werden immer die Themen aus mehreren Halbjahren (laut Erlass zwei Halbjahre) verbunden. Die folgende Übersicht soll es Ihnen erleichtern, sich bei der Vorbereitung auf die verbindlichen Prüfungsschwerpunkte zu konzentrieren:

Übersicht: verbindliche Themen Grundkurs

Q1 (12/I): The Challenge of Individualism
1. USA
   the American Dream, living together (ethnic groups: Hispanics), political life and issues, the U.S. and the world
2. Science and Technology
   biotechnology, electronic media, ecology

Q2 (12/II): Tradition and Change
1. United Kingdom
   social structures, social change, political life, political issues, Great Britain and the world (e.g. the British Empire, the Commonwealth)
2. Work and Industrialisation
   trade and competition, business, industry and the environment

Q3 (13/I): The Dynamics of Change
1. Promised Lands: Dreams and Realities (country of reference: Canada)
   ecology, political issues, social issues

2. Order, Vision, Change
   models of the future (utopias, dystopias, 'progress' in the natural sciences), revolt and revolution, world views, religion and sects, emancipation

Q4 (13/II): The Global Challenge (nicht relevant für das schriftliche Abitur)
1. Globalisation
   international division of labour, global economic structures vs. the nation state, fight for resources
2. Europe
   the EU, Europe and the world

Übersicht: verbindliche Themen Leistungskurs

Q1 (12/I): The Challenge of Individualism
1. USA
   the American Dream, living together (ethnic groups: Hispanics), political life and issues, the U.S. and the world
2. Them and Us
   the one-track mind, values, religion

Q2 (12/II): Tradition and Change
1. United Kingdom
   social structures, social change, political life, political issues and institutions, Great Britain and the world (e.g. the British Empire, the Commonwealth)
2. Extreme Situations
   love and happiness, fight for survival, tragic dilemma, the troubled mind

Q3 (13/I): The Dynamics of Change

1. Promised Lands: Dreams and Realities (countries of reference: e. g. Australia, Canada, New Zealand)
   new worlds/new horizons: modern utopias?, cultural traditions, political system/issues, social structure/issues, economic situation, ecology, international role
2. Ideals and Reality
   structural problems, structuring the world

Q4 (13/II): The Global Challenge (nicht relevant für das schriftliche Abitur)
1. Globalisation
   international division of labour, global economic structures vs. the nation state, fight for resources
2. Civil Society
   self-reliance and social commitment, NGOs vs. government responsibilities, privatization

Wie Sie der Liste entnehmen können, sind keine verbindlichen Lektüren vorgegeben. Der Erwartungshorizont der Abituraufgaben setzt jedoch voraus, dass Sie Bezüge zu literarischen Texten herstellen können (das können auch Kurzgeschichten, Romanauszüge oder Filme sein). Teilweise werden recht spezifische Kenntnisse erwartet. Deshalb sollten Sie die Themen sehr systematisch aufarbeiten und auch das entsprechende Fachvokabular einüben. Hierzu bieten Ihre Kursbücher sowie die dazugehörigen Workbooks oft gute Anregungen.

HINWEISE ZU DEN PRÜFUNGSBESTIMMUNGEN

Was sind Operatoren und Anforderungsbereiche?

Damit die Aufgabenstellung einheitlich und eindeutig ist, sind die sogenannten Operatoren eingeführt worden. Es handelt sich um eine Liste mit Bearbeitungsanweisungen, die Ihnen aus den Klausuren der Qualifikationsphase bekannt ist.

Die Operatoren sind drei Anforderungsbereichen zugeordnet: Anforderungsbereich I testet Ihr Textverständnis (meistens wird hier eine Inhaltsangabe verlangt). Diese Aufgabe zählt in der Regel 30 Prozent der Endnote. Anforderungsbereich II umfasst die Analyse des Textes und/oder den Vergleich mit vorher behandelten Texten und geht in der Regel mit 40 Prozent in die Endwertung ein. Im Anforderungsbereich III sind Sie aufgefordert, Ihre Meinung darzustellen und zu begründen. Dies kann auch im Rahmen einer kreativen Schreibaufgabe geschehen, z. B. in Form eines Leserbriefes oder einer Rede. Oft werden auch hier Querverbindungen zu anderen Kursthemen gezogen. Diese Aufgabe geht mit 30 Prozent in die Endwertung ein.

Operator	Definition	Beispiel
Anforderungsbereich I		
describe	give a detailed account of something	Describe the living conditions of the family.
outline	give the main features, structure or general principles of a topic omitting minor details	Outline the author's views on love, marriage and divorce.
point out	identify and explain certain aspects	Point out the author's main ideas on ...
summarise	give a concise account of the main points	Summarise the text (in your words).
Anforderungsbereich II		
analyse/ examine	systematically describe and explain in detail certain aspects and/or features of the text	Examine the author's use of language. Analyse the relationship between x and y.
characterise	describe and analyse the character(s)	Write a characterisation of the heroine.
compare	point out and analyse similarities and differences	Compare the living conditions described in the text with the idea of the "melting pot".
contrast/ juxtapose	describe and analyse the differences between two or more things	Contrast the author's concept of multiculturalism with concepts you have encountered in class.
explain	describe and define in detail	Explain the protagonist's obsession with money.
illustrate/ show	use examples to explain or make clear	Illustrate the character's narrow-mindedness.

Operator	Definition	Beispiel
relate	take an aspect/aspects of the text at hand and establish a meaningful connection to an aspect/aspects of the text of reference	Relate the protagonist's principles to a text read in class.
Anforderungsbereich III		
comment	state clearly your opinions on the topic in question and support your views with evidence	Comment on the thesis ... expressed in the text, line ...
discuss	analyse, give reasons for and against and come to a justified conclusion	Discuss the influence of terrorism on civil liberties in the United States.
evaluate/ assess	form an opinion after carefully considering and presenting advantages and disadvantages	Evaluate the chances of the protagonist's plan to succeed in life. Assess the importance of ethics in scientific research.
interpret	analyse the text and establish its meaning in a wider context	Interpret the message the author wishes to convey.

Wie gehe ich am besten an die Aufgaben heran und worauf sollte ich beim Bearbeiten achten?

Beginnen Sie möglichst frühzeitig mit Ihrer Vorbereitung und machen Sie sich einen Arbeitsplan. Zur Vorbereitung empfiehlt es sich, mit anderen zu lernen. Wenn Sie das Gelernte darstellen, fällt Ihnen auf, wo Sie Lücken haben, und außerdem können Sie sich gegenseitig unterstützen. Vermeiden Sie Stress in letzter Sekunde. Sie sollten sich am Prüfungstag möglichst ausgeruht in die Prüfung begeben (machen Sie vielleicht am Tag vorher Sport oder einen Spaziergang). Lassen Sie sich nicht kurz vor der Prüfung von Mitschülern verunsichern, sondern gehen Sie zuversichtlich in die Prüfung. Wenn Sie gut vorbereitet sind, werden Sie die Aufgaben auch bewältigen können.

Sichten Sie die drei Vorschläge zunächst kursorisch, denn vielleicht können Sie schon auf den ersten Blick einen Text aussortieren. Sie sollten nicht versuchen, alle drei Texte intensiv zu lesen, dabei verschenken Sie viel Zeit, die Sie später gut brauchen können. Wenn Sie Ihren Favoriten gefunden haben, lesen Sie den Text genau und machen Sie sich auf jeden Fall eine Lösungsskizze (in Form einer Gliederung oder einer Mindmap). Denken Sie daran, die im Unterricht behandelten Texte und Informationen möglichst klar und umfangreich in Ihre Antwort einzubringen. Aber spulen Sie keinesfalls nur das Gelernte ab, die Fakten müssen auch zur Fragestellung passen. Machen Sie sich zuvor einen Zeitplan für die Klausur.

Kommen Sie unbedingt zeitig zum Schluss, denn erstens häufen sich am Ende die Fehler und außerdem sollten Sie bei Unsicherheiten das Wörterbuch nutzen. Denken Sie daran, dass zwei Drittel der Note aus der sprachlichen Leistung resultieren, d. h., eine intensive sprachliche Korrektur wird sich auszahlen.

HINWEISE ZU DEN PRÜFUNGSBESTIMMUNGEN

Wie wird die Arbeit bewertet und wie viel zählt sie für die Endnote?

Ihre Klausur wird zunächst von Ihrer Englischlehrerin/Ihrem Englischlehrer begutachtet und dann einer zweiten Lehrkraft vorgelegt, die ihrerseits eine Bewertung abgibt. In der Regel ist der/die Zweitkorrektor/in eine Lehrkraft an Ihrer Schule, es können jedoch auch die Kollegien anderer Schulen herangezogen werden. Auskunft dazu, in welchen Fächern die Prüfungsarbeiten außer Haus zur Zweitkorrektur vorgelegt werden, gibt Ihre Schulleitung.

Die Bewertung der Abiturklausur weicht prinzipiell nicht von der Bewertung einer gewöhnlichen Klausur ab.

Im Fach Englisch werden drei Teilnoten erteilt auf sprachliche Richtigkeit, Stil und Inhalt, die jeweils zu einem Drittel in die Gesamtnote einfließen. Die Note für sprachliche Richtigkeit ist durch den Fehlerindex für die Stufen 12 und 13 verbindlich festgelegt. Hier fließen sowohl Wortfehler als auch grammatische Fehler und Rechtschreibfehler ein. Bei der Bewertung gilt die Liste über Fehlerindizes für die Qualifikationsphase (Fehler x 100 : Wortzahl).

Fehlerindex Grundkurs:

15	14	13	12	11	10	9	8
<0,9	−1,3	−1,7	−2,1	−2,5	−2,9	−3,3	−3,7

7	6	5	4	3	2	1	0
−4,1	−4,5	−4,9	−5,3	−5,7	−6,1	−6,5	>6,5

Fehlerindex Leistungskurs:

15	14	13	12	11	10	9	8
<0,7	−1,0	−1,3	−1,6	−1,9	−2,3	−2,6	−2,9

7	6	5	4	3	2	1	0
−3,2	−3,5	−3,8	−4,1	−4,4	−4,7	−5,0	>5,0

Den Stil bewertet Ihre Lehrerin/Ihr Lehrer nach den Kriterien Variation und Treffsicherheit des Vokabulars, Idiomatik, Vielfalt im Satzbau, Verbindung der Sätze und Paragrafen, stilistisch klarer Textaufbau, sprachlich korrekter und angemessener Ausdruck. Die inhaltliche Bewertung ist durch den Erwartungshorizont für die jeweilige Aufgabe festgelegt. Hier werden von Ihnen eine klare Darlegung Ihrer Gedanken sowie inhaltliche Richtigkeit und vielfältige Bezüge auf im Unterricht behandelte Themen erwartet.

Das Ergebnis der Prüfung wird vierfach gewertet, das Ergebnis des Grundkurses im Prüfungsfach in der 13/II geht einfach in die Abiturwertung ein, der Leistungskurs 13/II zählt doppelt.

Kann man sich noch mündlich prüfen lassen?

Eine zusätzliche mündliche Prüfung kann sowohl von der Prüfungskommission angeordnet als auch vom Schüler/von der Schülerin gewünscht werden. Falls Sie eine zusätzliche mündliche Prüfung ablegen möchten, müssen Sie das schriftlich beim Schulleiter/

bei der Schulleiterin beantragen. Sie können sich theoretisch in allen schriftlichen Prüfungsfächern auch mündlich prüfen lassen, sollten sich jedoch auf maximal ein zusätzliches Prüfungsfach beschränken. Eine zusätzliche Prüfung wird nicht gewährt, wenn es auch bei einer maximalen Punktzahl nicht mehr möglich ist, das Abitur zu bestehen. Sie kann auch verwehrt werden, wenn Sie nach Ablegen der schriftlichen Prüfungen das Abitur rechnerisch schon bestanden haben, aber durch eine Verschlechterung in der mündlichen Prüfung die Gefahr besteht, dass Sie durchfallen.

THE CHALLENGE OF INDIVIDUALISM

Trainingsaufgabe 1

Aufgabentyp	Comprehension, analysis, comment or re-creation of text (speech)
Thema	The challenge facing America
Material	Thomas L. Friedman: *The New 'Sputnik' Challenges: They All Run on Oil*. In: *The New York Times*
Textsorte	Sachtext
Niveau	Grundkurs und Leistungskurs

Assignments

1. Point out what Friedman says about the present challenges America has to face and what he considers the only possible way to meet them.

2. Examine how Friedman tries to convince his readers that action must be taken urgently to prevent "the decline of our way of life" (l. 56). Refer to the use of language and the argumentative techniques he employs.

3. Choose **one** of the following tasks:
   a) The author refers to the adaptation of the American Dream by the new global players India, China and the former Soviet Union (cf. ll. 25–27). Discuss whether their version of the American Dream can serve as a model in the 21st century, illustrating your view with examples of countries you have studied.

   or

   b) You are a guest student at an American college where Friedman's suggestion to introduce a gasoline tax is hotly debated among many of the students. One of your teachers makes you prepare a speech for or against this suggestion. Write a short speech to be held in class in which you refer to Friedman's article and argue from the perspective of a young European.

Material

Thomas L. Friedman
The New 'Sputnik' Challenges: They All Run on Oil

DETROIT – I came to Detroit looking for the hottest new American cars. Instead, I found Sputnik.
You remember Sputnik – the little satellite the Soviets launched in 1957. The Eisenhower administration was so stunned it put the U.S. into a crash program to train more scientists and engineers so America could catch up with the Russians in the space race. Well, for anyone paying attention, our generation's Sputnik showed up at the annual Detroit auto show this month. It's not a satellite. It's a car. It's called the Geely 7151 CK

Notizen

sedan. It seats a family of five, gets good mileage and will cost around $10,000 when it goes on sale in 2008. It's made in China.

That doesn't get your attention? Well, there's another Sputnik that just went up: Iran. It's going to make a nuclear bomb, no matter what the U.N. or U.S. says, because at $60-a-barrel oil, Tehran's mullahs are rich enough to buy off or tell off the rest of the world. That doesn't worry you? Well, there's a quieter Sputnik orbiting Earth. It's called climate change – a k a[1] Katrina[2] and melting glaciers.

What am I saying here? I am saying that our era doesn't have a single Sputnik to grab our attention and crystallize the threat to our security and way of life in one little steel ball – […]. But that doesn't mean such threats don't exist. They do, and they have a single common denominator: the way we use and consume energy today, particularly oil.

Friends, we are in the midst of an energy crisis – but this is not your grandfather's energy crisis. No, this is something so much bigger, for four reasons.

First, we are in a war against a radical, violent stream of Islam that is fueled and funded by our own energy purchases. We are financing both sides in the war on terrorism: the U.S. Army with our tax dollars, and Islamist charities, madrasas[3] and terrorist organizations through our oil purchases. Second, the world has gotten flat, and three billion new players from India, China and the former Soviet Union just walked onto the field with their version of the American dream: a house, a car, a toaster and a refrigerator. If we don't quickly move to renewable alternatives to fossil fuels, we will warm up, smoke up and choke up this planet far faster than at any time in the history of the world. Katrina will look like a day at the beach.

Third, because of the above, green energy-saving technologies and designs – for cars, planes, homes, appliances or office buildings – will be one of the biggest industries of the 21st century. Tell your kids. China is already rushing down this path because it can't breathe and can't grow if it doesn't reduce its energy consumption. Will we dominate the green industry, or will we all be driving cars from China, Japan and Europe? Finally, if we continue to depend on oil, we are going to undermine the whole democratic trend that was unleashed by the fall of the Berlin Wall. Because oil will remain at $60 a barrel and will fuel the worst regimes in the world – like Iran – to do the worst things for the world. Indeed, this $60-a-barrel boom in the hands of criminal regimes, and just plain criminals, will, if sustained, pose a bigger threat to democracies than communism or Islamism. It will be a black tide that turns back the democratic wave everywhere, including in Iraq.

The one thing we can do now to cope with all four of these trends is to create a tax that fixes the pump price at $3.50 to $4 a gallon[4] – no matter where the OPEC[5] price goes. Because if consumers know that the price of oil is never coming down, they will change their behavior. And when consumers change their behavior in a big way, G. M.[6], Ford and DaimlerChrysler will change their cars in a big way, and it is cars and trucks that consume a vast majority of the world's oil.

---

1 *abbreviation for* also known as
2 name of the hurricane that destroyed New Orleans in 2005
3 Islamic schools or seminaries in India and Pakistan that the US considers to be involved in planning and organizing terrorist attacks
4 ca. double the present American gasoline price and close to the European price level
5 Organization of Oil Exporting Countries, an organization of countries that produce and sell oil
6 General Motors, an American car-producing company

The more Detroit goes green, the faster it will be propelled down the innovation curve, making it more likely that Detroit – and not Toyota or Honda or the Chinese – will dominate the green technologies of the 21st century. A permanent gasoline tax will also make solar, wind and biofuels so competitive with oil that it will drive their innovations as well.

George Bush may think he is preserving the American way of life by rejecting a gasoline tax. But if he does not act now – starting with his State of the Union speech – he will be seen as the man who presided over the decline of our way of life. He will be the American president who ignored the Sputniks of our day.

(797 words)

Thomas L. Friedman: The New 'Sputnik' Challenges: They All Run on Oil. The New York Times, January 20, 2006, http://select.nytimes.com/2006/01/20/opinion/20friedman.html?hp

Lösungsvorschlag

Aufgabe 1

Point out what Friedman says about the present challenges America has to face and what he considers the only possible way to meet them.

Lösungsschritte

1. Markieren Sie im Text die relevanten Informationen zu den Herausforderungen, mit denen die Vereinigten Staaten konfrontiert sind, und zu Friedmans Lösungsansatz.
2. Formulieren Sie einen eigenständigen Text, in dem Sie die Probleme erklären und daraus die Lösung logisch ableiten. Verbinden Sie Ihre Gedanken durch Begriffe wie *this is why*, *because of this*, *this leads to*, *consequently*.
3. Lesen Sie Ihren Text erneut und verbessern Sie Fehler.

Stichpunktlösung

- Three challenges confronting America: rapid industrialisation, China, India (e.g. ll. 7–9, l. 26) – role of OPEC nations in Middle East, especially Iran, that could endanger US (e.g. ll. 10–12, ll. 22–25) – climate change, development of environmentally neutral technologies (e.g. ll. 13 f., ll. 27 f.),
- Friedman's conclusion: position of USA in a globalised world greatly weakened by dependence on oil, (ll. 18 f.),
- Friedman convinced USA must either charge a higher price for gasoline or levy a tax on gasoline to reduce its oil-dependence,
- Friedman expects two results: a) development of more economical cars by US car industry/Detroit, (ll. 47–49), b) encouragement/promotion of renewable energy (ll. 50–54).

Aufgabe 2

Examine how Friedman tries to convince his readers that action must be taken urgently to prevent "the decline of our way of life" (l. 56). Refer to the use of language and the argumentative techniques he employs.

Lösungsschritte

1. Markieren Sie beim erneuten Lesen alle Wendungen, die Ihnen auffallen, und überprüfen Sie, ob es sich um Metaphern oder Vergleiche, rhetorische Fragen oder Aufzählungen handelt. Wird der Leser direkt angesprochen, benutzt Friedman inklusive Personalpronomen (*we*), Wortspiele oder ein bestimmtes Wortfeld?
2. Verwendet der Autor leicht verständliche Alltagssprache oder ein spezialisiertes Fachvokabular?
3. Achten Sie auf den Aufbau der Rede – wie beginnt der Autor seine Paragrafen?
4. Schreiben Sie nun Ihre Analyse, in der Sie anhand der Textbeispiele belegen, welche rhetorischen Mittel Friedman wiederholt benutzt und welchen Effekt diese Stilmittel haben.
5. Korrigieren Sie beim erneuten Lesen Fehler.

THE CHALLENGE OF INDIVIDUALISM

Stichpunktlösung

- Sputnik metaphor: a) unexpected challenge that demanded a rapid reaction, b) structural function (title, introduction, conclusion),
- argumentation and/or structure: a) title (main focus of text, catching of reader's interest) b) structural/ordering devices: "First", "Second", "Third", "Finally",
- how Friedman speaks to reader: a) direct address, e. g. "You remember Sputnik" (l. 3), "… for anyone paying attention" (l. 6), "That doesn't get your attention?" (l. 10), b) use of first person personal pronouns we/our, c) use of language to create feelings of anxiety/insecurity: "the threat to our security" (l. 16), "the decline of our way of life" (l. 56), comparison between cold war/war on terrorism (l. 23),
- choice of language appropriate to a wide readership: a) informal, friendly tone, e. g. first person pronoun "I", "You/Friends", "catch up" (l. 5), "Well", "buy off or tell off" (l. 12) b) use of short sentences: "It's a car. It's called …" (l. 7), "Tell your kids". (l. 33) c) use of if-sentences with we: "If we don't quickly move to …, we will …" (ll. 27 f.), "if we continue to …, we are going to …" (ll. 36–38),
- stylistic devices used for emphasis: alliteration (l. 22), parallelism (ll. 7–9), metaphor (black tide, l. 41), enumeration (ll. 27 f.).

Aufgabe 3 a

The author refers to the adaptation of the American Dream by the new global players India, China and the former Soviet Union (cf. ll. 26–27). **Discuss** whether their version of the American Dream can serve as a model in the 21st century, illustrating your view with examples of countries you have studied.

Lösungsschritte

1. Legen Sie zunächst eine Stoffsammlung zum Thema an. Nennen Sie Fakten zum amerikanischen Traum. (Wie definiert ihn Friedman? Welche Aspekte kann es noch geben?) Welche Länder wollen Sie diskutieren (z. B. Indien)?
2. Gliedern Sie Ihre Notizen.
3. Beginnen Sie mit einer Einleitung. Hier empfiehlt es sich, zunächst kurz darzustellen, was der amerikanische Traum bedeutet (religiöse Wurzeln, Arbeitsethik, Überschreiten von Grenzen, schließlich Verengung auf persönlichen Erfolg und Reichtum = „a car, a house, a toaster and a refrigerator").
4. Wenden Sie diese Begriffe nun auf das Land Ihrer Wahl an. Stellen Sie dar, dass die BRIC-Staaten (Brasilien, Russland, Indien, China) als aufstrebende neue Wirtschaftsstaaten mit einer teilweise gut ausgebildeten jungen Bevölkerung und einem niedrigen Lohnniveau attraktive Standorte bieten und dies ein rasantes Wachstum generiert. Sie können sich auf Filme wie *Outsourced* beziehen.
5. Gehen Sie nun auf Probleme ein (Raubbau an Ressourcen, Nachhaltigkeit, Umweltverschmutzung, Klimawandel).
6. Stellen Sie in Ihrer Schlussfolgerung dar, welche Probleme Sie bei dieser Entwicklung sehen. Wenn möglich, können Sie auf Positivbeispiele verweisen (nachhaltige Landwirtschaft/Fair-Trade-Kooperativen).

Notizen

Stichpunktlösung

- (Asia/Eastern Europe): understanding of American Dream reduced to material goods alone; other aspects (freedom, pursuit of happiness ...) ignored, positive and negative results of a global American Dream based solely on consumption (house, car, washing-machine, toaster),
- consequences of spread of American Dream, e.g. to countries of Africa, Eastern Europe, Latin America,
- evaluation of arguments for and against as answer to question if the reduced (i.e. materialistic) American Dream can ever be practicable, realisable basis of a globalised world.

Aufgabe 3 b

You are a guest student at an American college where Friedman's suggestion to introduce a gasoline tax is hotly debated among many of the students. One of your teachers makes you prepare a speech for or against this suggestion. **Write** a short speech to be held in class in which you refer to Friedman's article and argue from the perspective of a young European.

Lösungsschritte

1. Machen Sie sich Notizen zum Thema *gasoline tax* – welche Vorteile/Nachteile sehen Sie? Welche Erfahrungen hat Deutschland damit gemacht? Sie können Argumente aus Friedmans Text verwenden.
2. Strukturieren Sie Ihre Rede in Einleitung, Hauptteil und Schluss.
3. Versuchen Sie durch rhetorische Mittel wie Metaphern, Wiederholungen, rhetorische Fragen u. Ä. Ihren Text ansprechend zu gestalten.
4. Lesen Sie den Text erneut und verbessern Sie Fehler.

Ausführliche Lösung

Suggestion for a speech:

My dear fellow students,
As some of you know, I am a guest student from Germany. I am honoured to have the opportunity of speaking to you this afternoon about environmental concerns from a European point of view.
I recently read that the economist Thomas L. Friedman thinks that the US government should introduce a tax on gasoline as the only way of reducing oil consumption.
Now, I know it is a difficult and even risky thing to speak as a guest in a foreign country on what seems a domestic matter such as this. However, as a European, I must tell you that we in Germany have had a heavy tax on fuel for decades. Today, over 70 % of the price of a litre of gasoline is tax.
Although some may complain about the size of the tax, nobody questions the principle. Is this, perhaps, because in densely-populated Europe we are more aware of environmental issues?
To begin with, I agree with Mr Friedman that our dependence on oil, much of which comes from the Middle East, means that we are faced with an absurd paradox. As he points out, we are both fighting terrorism with our taxes and financing it with our oil

imports. Is this acceptable? I hope you won't think me rude when I say, "No, it isn't". Secondly, huge countries like China, India and Brazil, which are in the process of industrialising, and others like the former Soviet Union and the countries of Eastern Europe obviously want to have their share of the world's resources and to become equal partners. And who can blame them? Aren't they just following our own example?

But the result of this understandable wish to enjoy a higher standard of living means that we are faced with a shortage of all forms of energy, most particularly oil.

With respect, in my opinion the only answer is that we must all, Americans and Europeans alike, consume much less energy ourselves and turn to renewable alternatives.

But I am convinced that we should not make the terrible mistake of looking at the question of oil-dependence from a narrowly economic point of view. To me, as a German, the issue of climate change caused by the burning of carbon fuels is still more important. This is surely the greatest danger facing us all, a much greater danger than that of international terrorism, for example.

The truth of the matter is, my friends, that if we don't do something – and do it now – nobody is going anywhere. Is that what we want for our children?

Notizen

26 THE CHALLENGE OF INDIVIDUALISM

Trainingsaufgabe 2

Aufgabentyp	Summary, comparison and letter to the editor (comment)
Thema	Illegal Immigration: Hispanics
Material	Embracing Illegals. In: *Business Week*
Textsorte	Sachtext
Niveau	Leistungskurs

Assignments

1. Summarise the Valenzuelas' story and explain how it became possible.
2. Compare the Valenzuelas' story to immigrant stories in Great Britain that you read in class.
3. Discuss whether US immigration policy should be liberalised or whether the current restrictions should be maintained in a letter to the editor of Business Week.

Material

Embracing Illegals
Companies are getting hooked on the buying power of 11 million undocumented immigrants

Inez and Antonio Valenzuela are a marketer's[1] dream. Young, upwardly mobile, and ready to spend on their growing family, the Los Angeles couple in many ways reflects the 42 million Hispanics in the U.S. Age 30 and 29, respectively, with two daughters, Esmeralda, 8, and Maria Luisa, 2 months, the duo puts in long hours, working 4 p.m. to
5   2 a.m., six days a week, at their bustling streetside taco trailer[2]. From a small sidewalk stand less than two years ago, they built the business into a hot destination for hungry commuters. The Valenzuelas (not their real name) bring in revenue[3] well above the U.S. household average of $43,000, making them a solidly middle-class family that any U.S. consumer-products company would love to reach.
10 But Inez and Antonio aren't your typical American consumers. They're undocumented immigrants who live and work in the U.S. illegally. When the couple, along with Esmeralda, crossed the Mexican border five years ago, they had little money, no jobs, and lacked basic documents such as Social Security numbers. Guided by friends and family, the couple soon discovered how to navigate[4] the increasingly above-ground world of
15 illegal residency. At the local Mexican consulate, the Valenzuelas each signed up for an

---
1 s.o. who sells goods or services
2 cheap mobile restaurant selling Mexican food
3 income
4 to find one's way; to understand or deal with sth. complicated

identification card known as a *matrícula consular,* for which more than half the applicants are undocumented immigrants, according to the Pew Hispanic center, a Washington think tank. Scores of financial institutions now accept it for bank accounts, credit cards, and car loans. Next, they applied to the Internal Revenue Service for individual tax identification numbers (ITINs), allowing them to pay taxes like any U.S. citizen – and thereby to eventually get a home mortgage[5].

Today, companies large and small eagerly cater to the Valenzuelas – regardless of their status. In 2003 they paid $11,000 for a used Ford Motor Co. van plus $70,000 more for a gleaming new 30-foot trailer that now serves as headquarters and kitchen for their restaurant. A local car dealer gave them a loan for the van based only on Antonio's *matrícula* card and his Mexican driver's license. Verizon Communications Inc. also accepted his *matrícula* when he signed up for cellphone service. So did a Wells Fargo & Co. branch in the predominantly Hispanic neighborhood in northeast Los Angeles where they live. Having a bank account allows them to pay bills by check and build up their savings. Their goal: to trade up[6] from a one-bedroom rental to their own home. Eventually, they also hope to expand their business by buying several more trailers. *Matrícula* holders like the Valenzuelas are "bringing us all the money that has been under the mattress", says Wells Fargo branch manager Steven Contreraz.

Growth Engine

(...)

The corporate Establishment's new hunger for the undocumenteds' business could have far-reaching implications for America's stance on[7] immigration policy, which remains unresolved. Corporations are helping, essentially, to bring a huge chunk of the underground economy into the mainstream. By finding ways to treat illegals like any other consumers, companies are in effect legalizing – and legitimizing – millions of people who technically have no right to be in the U.S. It's even happening in mirror image, with some Mexican companies setting up programs to follow customers who move to the U.S. All this knits the U.S. and Mexico closer together, further blurring the border and population distinctions.

The economic impact could be significant. While most analysts peg[8] the number of illegal immigrants at 10 million to 11 million, a recent study by Bear Stearns Asset Management concluded that data on housing permits, school enrollment, and foreign remittances[9] suggests there could be as many as 20 million. Either way, experts agree that the undocumented, a majority of whom are Hispanic, are one of the nation's largest sources of population growth. They add 700,000 new consumers to the economy every year, more even than the 600,000 or so legal immigrants, according to Pew's new study. What's more, 84% of illegals are 18-to-44-year-olds, in their prime spending years, vs. 60% of legal residents.

(677 words)

From: Business Week, July 18, 2005, pp. 43/44

---

5 a legal arrangement in which you borrow money from a bank in order to buy a house
6 to replace sth. you have with sth. better
7 attitude towards
8 to set sth. at a particular level
9 a sum of money that is sent to sb. (Geldüberweisung)

Lösungsvorschlag

Aufgabe 1

Summarise the Valenzuelas' story and explain how it became possible.

HINWEIS   Der Operator „summarise" erfordert eine knappe Schilderung der Lebensstationen der Valenzuelas. Achten Sie auf eine neutrale Darstellung der Situation. Benutzen Sie unbedingt eigene Worte.

Lösungsschritte

1. Markieren Sie relevante Informationen im Text.
2. Formulieren Sie einen einleitenden Satz (umbrella sentence), in dem Sie den Titel, die Quelle und das Thema nennen.
3. Ordnen Sie die Informationen und formulieren Sie die Antwort. Übernehmen Sie keine Satzfragmente aus dem Original, Ihr Text muss eigenständig sein.
4. Verbinden Sie Ihre Sätze und Paragrafen durch Konjunktionen wie *when*, *because*, *although*, *besides* usw.
5. Lesen Sie Ihre Antwort erneut durch und korrigieren Sie eventuelle Fehler. Achten Sie besonders darauf, das Simple Present zu benutzen.

Stichpunktlösung

- The Valenzuelas entered USA illegally from Mexico five years ago,
- now own small business – taco trailer,
- took advantage of semi-legal world of immigration; help of friends and family; obtained necessary documentation; *matrícula consular;* tax identification number,
- good financial standing; pay taxes; obtained loans for trailer, cellphone contract,
- earn more than the average American family; attractive to American economy,
- The Valenzuelas made a life for themselves in the USA.

HINWEIS   Erstellen Sie nun eine ausführliche Lösung.

Aufgabe 2

Compare the Valenzuelas' story to immigrant stories in Great Britain that you read in class.

Lösungsschritte

1. Lesen Sie den vorliegenden Text nochmals aufmerksam. Für die erste Aufgabe haben Sie bereits die relevanten Informationen über die Valenzuelas herausgeschrieben. Benutzen Sie diese als Grundlage für den Vergleich.
2. Machen Sie sich Notizen zu vergleichbaren Situationen in den Büchern oder Filmen, die Sie im Unterricht besprochen haben. Neben *The Buddha of Suburbia*, der hier in der Stichpunktlösung herangezogen wird, könnten Sie sich auch auf Filme wie *East is East* oder *My Beautiful Laundrette* beziehen.
3. Verfassen Sie nun Ihren Text und denken Sie daran, die genannten Aspekte miteinander zu vergleichen, wobei Parallelen und Unterschiede klar dargestellt werden sollten. Benutzen Sie dabei Redemittel zur Strukturierung wie *compared to*, *in contrast to*, *however* usw.
4. Stellen Sie in der Schlussfolgerung nochmals die wichtigsten Aspekte dar.
5. Lesen Sie den Text erneut und verbessern Sie Fehler. Achten Sie dabei besonders auf die Wortstellung und die Zeitformen der Verben.

Stichpunktlösung

Valenzuelas	Immigrants to Great Britain in *The Buddha of Suburbia*
Background information: ■ They are illegal immigrants who came across the Mexican-American border. ■ There are between 10 and 20 million illegal residents in the US. ■ Presumably they were poor in Mexico and came to the US to find a better standard of living by working hard (pursuit of happiness). ■ 84 percent of illegals are between 18 and 44 years old – a considerable marketforce.	**Background information:** ■ Many British immigrants are legal citizens from Commonwealth countries. ■ Unlike the Valenzuelas they need not fear being discovered and the question of whether they can do business legally does not arise.

THE CHALLENGE OF INDIVIDUALISM

Valenzuelas	Immigrants to Great Britain in *The Buddha of Suburbia*
■ The Valenzuelas live and work in the US, their children go to school etc. all without official documents. ■ They have a business of their own, which earns good money. ■ They have invested in the US by buying a van and a taco trailer, they hope to save up their money to buy their own home in the future.	■ The Valenzuelas can be compared to Uncle Anwar and Auntie Jeeta. ■ Being from a middle or upper class background in India, where they had servants and played cricket, Anwar and Haroon come to Britain to get a good education and then return to India as accomplished gentlemen, Anwar's wife Jeeta is even a princess.
■ This is why companies are interested in attracting young families to their branches and thereby legitimise illegal immigrants. ■ While Hispanics are met with prejudice and sometimes hatred in the US too, this is not the topic in this text. Neither is the fear of being discovered and sent home.	■ In fact Haroon does not know how to prepare a meal or clean his shoes as this was done by servants at home. ■ Arriving in Britain they are shocked by food rationing and by meeting British workers, who do not wash regularly and have no desire to discuss poetry. ■ After studying in Britain Anwar opens a corner shop, which can be compared to the Valenzuelas' taco trailer. However, unlike the Valenzuelas he wins the money by betting on horses. So there is no real hard work involved in his start-up. ■ Unlike the Valenzuelas, Uncle Anwar and Haroon have come to Britain hoping to find a more sophisticated life without hard work. ■ Haroon stays true to this, disdaining money and looking for the true meaning of life in Chinese philosophy and yoga.

Conclusion:

■ There is a difference in the social background of the Valenzuelas (presumably working class) and Uncle Anwar (upper middle class) and their expectations. While the Valenzuelas seem to have known what they were letting themselves in for, the two Indians are shocked and surprised by the real life they encounter. Unlike the Valenzuelas they are not used to hard work and do not expect to have to earn a living.

Notizen

LÖSUNG: TRAININGSAUFGABE 2

Aufgabe 3

Discuss whether US immigration policy should be liberalised or whether the current restrictions should be maintained in a letter to the editor of Business Week.

HINWEIS   Der Operator ist hier „discuss", d. h., Sie müssen Stärken und Schwächen der jetzigen Politik darstellen und dann erklären, ob Sie eine Liberalisierung für sinnvoll halten. Geben Sie unbedingt Gründe für Ihre Meinung an. Denken Sie an die korrekte Anrede *(Dear Madam/Dear Sir oder To Whom It May Concern)* und Schlussformel *(Yours faithfully oder Best regards)*.

Lösungsschritte

1. Erstellen Sie eine Stoffsammlung mit Informationen zur Immigrationspolitik der USA. Stellen Sie Stärken und Schwächen dar.
2. Formulieren Sie eine Einleitung, hierbei können Sie sich auf aktuelle Fälle, statistische Informationen oder auch literarische Figuren beziehen (z. B. aus T. C. Boyles *The Tortilla Curtain*).
3. Verfassen Sie nun den Brief. Achten Sie auf eine strukturierte Darstellung, nennen Sie Vor- und Nachteile und beziehen Sie sich auf Beispiele aus dem Unterricht
4. Lesen Sie Ihre Antwort erneut durch und verbessern Sie Fehler.

Stichpunktlösung

Suggestion for the letter
Dear Sir/Madam,
At last, at last, somebody has realised the positive impact immigration can have on our society. I was very pleased to read the article "Embracing Illegals" in the July 18 edition. For far too long this country has been told that immigration from South and Central America must be stopped. Aren't we a country that has been built by immigrants from all over the world? What would have happened, for example, if American policy had stopped Irish immigration in the 19th and 20th century? We would not be famous for the Model T – Henry Ford was of Irish origin – and Kennedy, also of Irish ancestry, would not have been our president. American culture and American society would be poorer and probably even more boring without the steady influx of new cultures, ideas and people who are willing to work hard and make a living here. The same must be true for immigration from South and Central America and, finally, people – or, more importantly, the economy – are beginning to understand that. This is an important step towards the liberalisation of immigration laws, which is badly needed. We don't need a wall between Mexico and the USA, we need politicians that make laws to help immigrants to build their lives here and to contribute to this "melting pot" that is the USA.
Best regards

SCIENCE AND TECHNOLOGY

Trainingsaufgabe 3

Aufgabentyp	Summary, rhetorical analysis, re-creation of text (speech)
Thema	Genetic Engineering
Material	Auszug aus Naomi Klein: *Fences and Windows*
Textsorte	Sachtext
Niveau	Grundkurs

Assignments

1. Summarize the text.

2. Show how Naomi Klein gets her critical attitude across to the reader.

3. a) You are to give a speech to 'Young Entrepreneurs', a group of young businesspeople in your community, on the relationship between profit-making and the environmental and health concerns of the population. Title: "They call it 'Frankenfood', we call it 'Healthfood': Free research and competition lead to a better future."

   or

   b) You are to give a speech to the local chapter of 'Greenpeace', on the relationship between profit-making and the environmental and health concerns of the population. Title: "They call it 'Healthfood', we call it 'Frankenfood': On the dangers of the business mentality."

Material

Naomi Klein
You can't eat public relations (August 2000)

"This rice could save a million kids a year." That was the arresting headline on the cover of last week's *Time* magazine. It referred to golden rice, a newly market-ready variety of genetically engineered grain that contains extra beta carotene, which helps the body produce vitamin A. All over Asia, millions of malnourished children suffer from vitamin A deficiency, which can lead to blindness and death.
To get their supposed miracle cure off the ground, AstraZeneca, the company that owns marketing rights for golden rice, has offered to donate the grains to poor farmers in countries such as India, where genetically engineered crops have so far met fierce resistance. [...]

10 GE¹ foods, originally greeted with rubber stamps² from governments and indifference from the public, have rapidly become an international repository for anxiety [...]. Opponents argue that the current testing standards fail to take into account the complex web of interrelations that exists among living things. Altered soybeans, for example, may appear safe in a controlled test environment, but how, once grown in nature, will
15 they affect the weeds around them, the insects that feed on them and the crops that cross-pollinate with them?
What has blindsided the agribusiness companies is that the fight has been a battle of the brands as much as one of warring scientific studies. Early on, activists decided to aim their criticism not at agribusiness itself but at the brandname supermarkets and
20 packaged-food companies that sold products containing "Frankenfoods."
Their brand images tarnished, British supermarkets began pulling products off their shelves, and companies such as Gerber and Frito-Lay went GE-free. In the United States and Canada, environmentalists have set their sights on Kellogg's and Campbell's Soup, parodying their carefully nurtured logos and costly ad campaigns.
25 At first, the agribusiness companies couldn't figure out how to respond. Even if they could claim that their altered foods had no harmful effects, they couldn't point to direct nutritional benefits either. So that raised the question, Why take a risk? Which is where golden rice comes in. AstraZeneca now has a benefit to point to – not to mention a powerful brand of its own to fight the brand wars with.
30 Golden rice has all the feel-good ingredients of a strong brand. First, it's golden, as in golden retrievers and gold cards and golden sunsets. Second, unlike other genetically engineered foods, it isn't spliced with ghastly fish genes but rather melded with sunny daffodils. [...]
There are plenty of low-tech solutions to vitamin A deficiency. Programs already exist
35 to encourage the growth of diverse, vitamin-rich vegetables on small plots, yet the irony of these programs (which receive little international support) is that their task is not to invent a sexy new sci-fi food source. It's to undo some of the damage created the last time Western companies and governments sold an agricultural panacea³ to the developing world.
40 During the so-called Green Revolution, small-scale peasant farmers, growing a wide variety of crops to feed their families and local communities, were pushed to shift to industrial, export-oriented agriculture. That meant single, high-yield crops, produced on a large scale. Many peasants, now at the mercy of volatile commodity prices and deep in debt to the seed companies, lost their farms and headed for the cities. In the
45 countryside, meanwhile, severe malnutrition exists alongside flourishing "cash crops" such as bananas, coffee and rice. Why? Because in children's diets, as in the farm fields, diverse foods have been replaced with monotony. A bowl of white rice is lunch and dinner.
The solution being proposed by the agribusiness giants? Not to rethink mono-crop farm-
50 ing and fill that bowl with protein and vitamins. They want to wave another magic wand and paint the white bowl golden.

(618 word)

Reprinted by permission of HarperCollins Publishers Ltd. © 2004 Naomi Klein

1 genetically engineered (genetic engineering)
2 gladly and speedily
3 Allheilmittel

SCIENCE AND TECHNOLOGY

Lösungsvorschlag

Aufgabe 1

Summarize the text.

HINWEIS   Benutzen Sie das Simple Present und denken Sie daran, einen einleitenden Satz (*umbrella sentence*) zu formulieren.

Lösungsschritte

1. Unterstreichen Sie die Kernpunkte (keine Details, Beispiele, wörtliche Rede, Aufzählung).
2. Formulieren Sie einen einleitenden Satz, in dem Sie Autorin, Quelle und Thema nennen.
3. Lösen Sie sich vom Text und formulieren Sie eine kurze Zusammenfassung in eigenen Worten (im Simple Present). Achten Sie darauf, dass die logischen Zusammenhänge deutlich werden, indem Sie Verbindungswörter benutzen.

Ausführliche Lösung

The text "You can't eat public relations" by Naomi Klein is an excerpt from her book *Fences and Windows*. Naomi Klein is a well-known critic of globalization, and in this text she criticizes the promotion of a new type of genetically modified rice and calls for more sustainable and small-scale solutions to solve the problem of malnutrition.
AstraZeneca claim their new GE rice ("golden rice") could save children from the results of vitamin A deficiency. The company is willing to donate grains to poor farmers and thus overcome their resistance to GE seeds.
Then Klein goes on to explain that GE foods are frequently criticized because their long-term consequences for the complex environmental balance cannot be tested. In the past activists focussed on certain brands which used GE crops, and this strategy has been successful as consumers are unwilling to take risks with their food. Today AstraZeneca has devised a new strategy. Apart from using a strong brand they promote a GE product which has a benefit to offer.
Finally the author calls for more sustainable solutions and advises small-scale farming of diverse crops instead of monocultures which have made farmers dependent on world market prices and driven them into debt, but agribusinesses are blind to their mistakes.

(208 words)

Aufgabe 2

Show how Naomi Klein gets her critical attitude across to the reader.

HINWEIS   Es geht um eine Analyse der Leserlenkung im Text. Hierbei werden Sie sich auf die Sprache und die Verwendung von Stilmitteln konzentrieren müssen. Achten Sie darauf, die Stilmittel nicht nur korrekt zu benennen und mit Zitaten zu belegen, sondern erläutern Sie deren Wirkung auf die Leserschaft.

Notizen

Lösungsschritte

1. Lesen Sie den Text nochmals aufmerksam und markieren Sie auffällige Wendungen und verwendete Stilmittel (rhetorische Frage, Metaphern, Alliteration, Aufzählung usw.). Welche Wirkung haben sie auf die Leser?
2. Welches sprachliche Register wird verwendet? Wer sind die Leser?
3. Formulieren Sie nun Ihre Analyse und strukturieren Sie diese in Paragrafen.
4. Achten Sie darauf, durch Mittel zur Textstrukturierung geeignete Überleitungen zu schaffen.
5. Lesen Sie Ihren Text nochmals genau durch, verbessern Sie Sprache und Stil.

Stichpunktlösung

- Klein is critical of GE foods and large multinational companies,
- readers: interested in issue of globalisation,
- language: uses partly specific vocabulary, but generally not too difficult,
- start: catchy quote to arouse reader's curiosity: "This rice could save a million kids a year." (l. 1),
- words to shed doubt on industry's claim: "supposed miracle" (l. 6), "so-called Green Revolution" (l. 40),
- new word to catch attention and arouse fear: "Frankenfoods" (l. 20) = allusion to Dr Frankenstein, who created a monster.

Variety of stylistic devices to convince the readers:
- Parallelism to criticize lack of earlier reaction both on the part of governments and the public: "greeted with rubber stamps from governments and indifference from the public" (ll. 10–11),
- rhetorical question: "[…] but how, once grown in nature, will they affect the weeds around them, the insects that feed on them and the crops that cross-pollinate with them?" (ll. 14–16) to show that nobody can have those answers yet and GE food poses incalculable risks,
- enumerations:
  - "the weeds around them, the insects that feed on them and the crops that cross-pollinate with them?" (ll. 15–16) to show how the complex web of nature is affected by GE crops,
  - "golden retrievers and gold cards and golden sunsets" (l. 31) to point out examples of positive associations for 'golden' but also to point to a marketing strategy: whereas golden retrievers and golden sunsets are part of nature, a 'gold card' already uses the positive connotations of 'gold' to market a product,
- metaphors focussed on war to underline the fierce quality of the dispute: "the battle of the brands" (ll. 17–18), "warring scientific studies" (l. 18), "to fight the brand wars" (l. 29),
- metaphor to show how unrealistic firms' GE policies are: "They want to wave another magic wand and paint the white bowl golden." (ll. 50–51),
- metonymy (pars pro toto): "a bowl of white rice" (l. 47) for monotonous diet,
- bowl recurs in the following paragraph: "fill that bowl with protein and vitamins" (l. 50) to show what should be done (provide a more diverse and healthier diet) and "paint the white bowl golden" (l. 51) for what the companies plan to do (replace their former policies of monocultures with GE crops),

SCIENCE AND TECHNOLOGY

- alliterations: "battle of the brands" (ll. 17–18), "deep in debt" (l. 44) to make expressions more memorable.

Aufgabe 3 a

You are to give a speech to 'Young Entrepreneurs', a group of young businesspeople in your community, on the relationship between profit-making and the environmental and health concerns of the population. Title: "They call it 'Frankenfood', we call it 'Healthfood': Free research and competition lead to a better future."

Lösungsschritte

1. Machen Sie sich Notizen zu den Argumenten und Beispielen, die Sie verwenden wollen, um Ihre Position deutlich zu machen. Auch in einer Rede müssen Sie Ihre Thesen argumentativ durch Beispiele, Statistiken oder Zitate belegen. Strukturieren Sie Ihre Rede.
2. Denken Sie daran, im einleitenden Satz die Hörer zu begrüßen und für die Einladung zu danken. Nennen Sie zu Beginn das Thema Ihrer Rede.
3. Verlieren Sie das Thema nicht aus den Augen – konzentrieren Sie sich auf die Diskussion der Schlüsselwörter.
4. Achten Sie beim Schreiben darauf, Stilmittel zu verwenden, um die Aufmerksamkeit auf Kernpunkte zu lenken und die Zuhörer zu überzeugen.
5. Formulieren Sie einen abschließenden Absatz, der in Reden oft eine Handlungsaufforderung enthält.

Ausführliche Lösung

Dear colleagues

Thanks for the invitation to speak at your convention today. I am especially grateful to meet so many young, dedicated and talented entrepreneurs who are bent on making our economy more modern and our future more secure. My topic today is: "Free research and competition lead to a better future." And this is what we are all concerned about – how to make the future beneficial, how to make it brighter, how to make it better for everyone.

Some people say, "Striving for profit is bad." They claim that it damages environmental standards, especially when it comes to GE food developments. Now this is a very shortsighted way of arguing. In fact it is also an oversight on the part of the speaker. It may be true that in the past some companies have put profit before the environment, sometimes with catastrophic consequences. But you are not the entrepreneurs of yesteryear. We are young and we understand the relevance of protecting the environment for our future. This future is our own future and we are concerned to make it a healthy and safe future.

Before we hit the market with new products, especially where GE foods are concerned, we spend a lot of our time and resources on carefully investigating the consequences of new developments. Some environmentalists will ask, "But how can you know these consequences?" Our models and analyses allow us to make precise predictions on how a certain GE grain will behave. And we know for sure that it is a way to make harvests secure. GE grains are resistant to droughts or heavy rains and they can withstand bugs which so often ruin the harvest of a whole year. In fact we can guarantee richer and

Notizen

safer harvests. And these are harvests which can do without harmful pesticides as the grains themselves are so much more advanced. At a time when the world population is predicted to rise to 9 billion within the next 40 years, this is no mean feat. I would say more, it is a necessity to invest in these technologies now, as they not only promise a profitable future, they promise a peaceful future, a future when nobody will suffer from hunger or malnutrition, a future when nobody will fight bloody wars about food for their children.

In order to develop new GE foods and to make them marketable, we need unrestricted conditions for our research. If our country cannot provide those conditions, young entrepreneurs and young scientists will move elsewhere and we will be left out. We will be left behind. It will be more forward-looking countries that reap a rich harvest.

Other critics say, "Competition is bad." They claim competition destroys jobs and damages working conditions. They yearn for a security which – frankly speaking – is a thing that never existed, except perhaps the deceptive security of socialism, where people felt free to leave their workplace and stand in line for a loaf of bread for hours. Is this the type of lifestyle we strive for? I don't think so.

Why, I ask you, should competition be bad? On the contrary, competition is healthy, competition encourages us to think in new and unaccustomed ways and to develop fresh products. Let me tell you, competition is a fact of life and it awakens our better instincts, our ambitions and our dreams. It drives us to work faster and more creatively. And if we do this, we won't lag behind international developments. We will be up there with the most innovative and the best firms on the globe.

This is why we are here today, to look ahead into a more creative, a brighter and a fairer future with our products competing on the world market and jobs secure. This is a future worth fighting for. It is a future we can all look forward to. Thank you.

(645 words)

Aufgabe 3 b

You are to give a speech to the local chapter of 'Greenpeace', on the relationship between profit-making and the environmental and health concerns of the population. Title: "They call it 'Healthfood', we call it 'Frankenfood': On the dangers of the business mentality."

HINWEIS   Gehen Sie bei dieser Aufgabe genauso vor wie in Aufgabe 3a und befolgen Sie die dort beschriebenen Lösungsschritte.

Ausführliche Lösung

Dear friends

Thank you for your invitation to talk to you today about the dangers of the business mentality. I am going to talk to you about marketing potentially dangerous foods for a maximum profit by disguising them as healthy. They call it 'Healthfood', they claim their rice can save a million kids from blindness and death every year. They promise to provide children with more beta carotene, which will help them to produce vitamin A. But I say it is they who are blind. They are blind to the dangers of their product. They have been blinded by the promise of a million dollars and more to be made from selling this product to hapless farmers all over the world. They do not want to save all those children from blindness, they want to make them dependent on their new type of crop and lead them to another type of blindness altogether: the blindness of a herd of so-called business people who follow where dollars are promised.

What is their product? A type of grain which has been genetically modified in a laboratory. A type of grain that works well in the sterile conditions of high-tech labs in California. A type of grain that promises undreamt of profit margins if only they manage to sell it to a million farmers in Africa and southern Asia. But this is not the type of grain which a million starving children in the developing world have been waiting for. No, my dear friends, this is the type of grain which will make poor farmers dependent on a foreign company which is not familiar with the traditional ways of farming used in these parts of the world. They promote their new GE crops in the poorest countries and sell them to farmers there. Farmers who can barely afford to buy those high-tech products and who will get into debt, trying to finance this new investment. And then they will be faced with a new kind of dependency. The dependency on the providers of their new crop, who will dictate their business policies and who can raise their prices at will. And who will undoubtedly do so to finance their research and then maximize their profit.

We have seen it before during the Green Revolution. What came along as a promise for a brighter and better future turned out to be a massive failure, which drove small farmers into debt and forced them to sell their land and move to the slums in the new megalopolises. This Green Revolution made millions of farmers landless, homeless and hopeless. To call it green – the colour of green fields and of hope – is ironic. It should be called the Mean Revolution, mean like the managers of the companies bent on profit above all else.

One last question: You may wonder if there are no hidden benefits in GE developments. Should not scientists be allowed to pursue their science? Will this not be beneficial to society? We know of many scientists who followed their science blindly. One of them was Mary Shelley's famous Frankenstein, who was blinded by his ambition to make life and in fact created a monster. Frankenstein is a protagonist of fiction. The book sends shivers down our spines when we read about his endeavours. But he is also a powerful personification of the scientist who is blind to the consequences of his science and who, when he is faced with them, is overcome by helpless terror and must wander the world to undo what he has created. Frankenstein is a tragic story, as the story of Robert D. Oppenheimer and his colleagues in the Manhattan Project, fathers of the atomic bombs which destroyed millions of lives in Hiroshima and Nagasaki. Potentially tragic as the story of those scientists who developed 'golden rice' and marketed it to the world. This last story is one that can still be turned into a happy one if we work together to inform people and to fight the ruthless business strategies of companies such as AstraZeneca.

We are not here today to talk, we are here to act. Act as responsible citizens of the world, fighters for a better future. Let us not be blinded and numbed. Let us get up and get our hands dirty. Let's fight the good fight. Thank you.

(724 words)

Notizen

Trainingsaufgabe 4

Aufgabentyp	Comprehension, interpretation and comparison, discussion
Thema	Religion and science
Material	Suzanne Goldenberg: *Religious right fights science for the heart of America*. In: *The Guardian* Patrick Hardin: *What's it all about?* (Cartoon)
Textsorte	Sachtext
Niveau	Leistungskurs

Assignments

1. Outline how religion influences teaching.
2. Interpret the cartoon and compare it to the text.
3. There should be no ethical limits to science. Discuss.

Material 1

Suzanne Goldenberg
Religious right fights science for the heart of America

Al Frisby has spent the better part of his life in rooms filled with rebellious teenagers, but the last years have been particularly trying for the high school biology teacher. He has met parents who want him to teach that God created Eve out of Adam's rib, and who insist that Noah invited dinosaurs aboard the ark. And it is getting more difficult
5 to keep such talk out of the classroom.
"Somewhere along the line, the students have been told the theory of evolution is not valid," he said. "In the last few years, I've had students question my teaching about cell classification and genetics, and there have been comments from students saying: Didn't God do that?" In Kansas, the geographical centre of America, the heart of the American
10 heartland, the state-approved answer might soon be Yes. In the coming weeks, state educators will decide on proposed curriculum changes for high school science put forward by subscribers to the notion of "intelligent design", a modern version of creationism. If the religious right has its way, and it is a powerful force in Kansas, high school science teachers could be teaching creationist material by next September.
15 Similar classroom confrontations between God and science are under way in 17 states, according to the National Centre for Science Education. In Missouri, state legislators are drafting a bill laying down that science texts contain a chapter on so-called alternative theories to evolution. Textbooks in Arkansas and Alabama contain disclaimers on evolution, and in a Wisconsin school district, teachers are required to instruct their stu-
20 dents in the "scientific strengths and weaknesses of evolutionary theory". Last month, a judge in Georgia ordered a school district to remove stickers on school textbooks that

warned: "This textbook contains material on evolution. Evolution is a theory, not a fact, regarding the origin of living things."

For the conservative forces engaged in the struggle for America's soul, the true battleground is public education, the laboratory of the next generation, and an opportunity for the religious right to effect lasting change on popular culture. Officially, the teaching of creationism has been outlawed since 1987 when the Supreme Court ruled that the inclusion of religious material in science classes in public teaching was unconstitutional. In recent years, however, opponents of evolution have regrouped, challenging science education with the doctrine of "intelligent design", which has been carefully stripped of all references to God and religion. Unlike traditional creationism, which posits that God created the earth in six days, proponents of intelligent design assert that the workings of this planet are too complex to be ascribed to evolution. There must have been a designer working to a plan – that is, a creator.

In their campaign to persuade parents in Kansas to welcome the new version of creationism into the classroom, subscribers to intelligent design have appealed to a sense of fair play, arguing that it would be in their children's interest to be exposed to all schools of thought on the earth's origins. "We are looking for science standards that would be more informative, that would open the discussion about origins, rather than close it," said John Calvert, founder of the Intelligent Design network.

Other supporters of intelligent design go further, saying evolution is as much an article of faith as creationism. "Certainly there are clear religious implications," said William Harris, a research biochemist and co-founder of the design network in Kansas. "There are creation myths on both sides. Which one do you teach?" During the past five years, subscribers to intelligent design have assembled influential supporters in the state, including a smattering of people with PhDs, such as Mr Harris, to lend their cause a veneer of scientific credibility. When conservative Republicans took control of the Kansas state school board, the creationists seized their chance, installing supporters on the committee reviewing the high school science curriculum.

Jack Krebs, a high school maths teacher on the committee drafting the new standards, argues that the campaign against evolution amounts to a stealth assault on the entire body of scientific thought. "There are two planes where they are attacking. One is evolution, and one is science itself," he said. "They believe that the naturalist bias of science is in fact atheistic. And so this is really an attack on all of science."

It would certainly seem so in Kansas. At the first of a series of public hearings on the new course material, the audience was equally split between the defenders of established science and the anti-evolution rebels. In a crowded high school auditorium, biology teachers, mathematicians, a veterinarian, and a high school student made passionate speeches on the need for cold, scientific detachment, and the damage that would be done to the state's reputation and biotechnology industry if Kansas became known as a haven for creationists. They were countered by John James, who warned that the teaching of evolution led to nihilism, and to the gates of Auschwitz. But the largest applause of the evening was reserved for a silver-haired gentleman. "I have a question: if man comes from monkeys, why are there still monkeys? Why do you waste time teaching something in science class that is not scientific?" he thundered.

Science teachers believe that the genteel questioning of the intelligent design movement masks a larger project to discredit an entire body of rational thought. If the Kansas state school board allows science teachers to question evolution, where will it stop? Will religious teachers bring their beliefs into the classroom?

"They are trying to create a climate where anything an individual teacher wants to include in science class can be considered science," said Harry McDonald, a retired biology teacher and president of Kansas Citizens for Science Education. "They want to redefine science."

Suzanne Goldenberg: Religious right fights science for the heart of America. In: The Guardian, february 7, 2005. Copyright Guardian News & Media Ltd 2005

Material 2

From: galleri.magiskamolekyler.org © 1993 by Patrick Hardin. www.CartoonStock.com

Lösungsvorschlag

Aufgabe 1

Outline how religion influences teaching.

Lösungsschritte

1. Unterstreichen Sie die relevanten Passagen im Text.
2. Ordnen Sie die Informationen, beginnend mit dem historischen Kontext (Verbot religiöser Ansichten im Jahre 1987).
3. Formulieren Sie einen eigenständigen Text, in dem Sie die Einflussnahme der religiösen Gruppen auf die Schule darstellen.
4. Lesen Sie Ihren Text erneut und verbessern Sie Fehler.

Stichpunktlösung

- After being outlawed in 1987, religious material is being included in science curricula again,
- in 17 states conservative Christian groups have started to exert their influence on state legislation in order to change the science curriculum to include intelligent design,
- intelligent design is a modern form of creationism, it says that a higher intelligence must have shaped the complex forms of life on earth, but it does not call this higher intelligence God,
- they argue that a scientific debate should contain all sorts of materials and theories, including religious ones,
- in their view, evolution is a kind of religion as well,
- they have influential supporters in some scientists and a number of Republican politicians to give them credibility,
- Jack Krebs argues that this is an attack on the naturalist approach to all sciences,
- Kansas: curriculum changes under way to include intelligent design in science classes,
- Missouri: textbooks must include chapters on alternative theories to evolution,
- Arkansas and Alabama: disclaimers on evolution required in textbooks,
- Georgia: stickers on science textbooks describing evolution as a theory, not a fact, had to be removed by court orders.

Aufgabe 2

Interpret the cartoon and compare it to the text. Refer to the role religion has traditionally played in the United States.

Lösungsschritte

1. Beginnen Sie damit, dass Sie das Thema der Karikatur nennen.
2. Beschreiben Sie anschließend den Cartoon in allen Details, das bedeutet, alle Figuren, ihr Aussehen, ihre Gedanken, und ordnen Sie diese in den Kontext Evolution/Religion ein.

3. Interpretieren Sie die Aussage des Cartoons und stellen Sie Bezüge zum Text her.
4. Erläutern Sie dann die Rolle der Religion in den Vereinigten Staaten.

Ausführliche Lösung

The cartoon by Patrick Hardin shows the different stages in the evolution of man and it claims that the main thing that has changed is the fact that humans strive to find the meaning of life. On the left we can see a kind of fish leaving the water, showing the important evolutionary step from water to land. The main purpose of life for this creature is "eat, survive, reproduce" as the thought bubble says. These three points are vital for successful survival and evolution. Animals must eat, they must protect themselves from enemies and harmful influences to survive and only if they reproduce, can their race go on existing. The second animal is a kind of lizard or dinosaur and it has the same priorities, "eat, survive, reproduce." The third animal is similar to the second, it has only slightly changed in appearance and it has the same ideas, "eat, survive, reproduce." The fourth animal is a kind of ape with the same thoughts. In the fifth evolutionary step we can see a human being, walking on two legs and fully dressed. The man has his hands in his pockets and he is wondering "What's it all about?" This shows that man is searching for a deeper meaning, eating, surviving and reproducing as basic functions of evolution is not enough. This is where both religion and science come in. Religion gives a spiritual dimension to life in answering the existential questions "where do we come from?", "where do we go?", "why do we exist?". Funnily the cartoon also answers two of these questions as according to science, we have evolved from simple organisms and we are here to "eat, survive and reproduce". Animals know this instinctively, but man is worrying unnecessarily. So we can say the cartoon is making fun of man's quest for meaning, that is religion.

The text is about including intelligent design in teaching science in the United States. We are told that in some states Fundamentalist Christian groups are trying to convince educators to include teaching that a higher intelligence created life in their science lessons and to treat evolution as just one theory among many. This movement is discrediting evolution and all its scientific evidence as an explanation for why human life has developed and wants to include a religious theory in the science curriculum. It is like the man on the right hand side of the cartoon, who is asking himself why he is here, even though he has evolved from the animals through scientifically proved stages. And if he is a Fundamentalist Christian, his answer will leave out this scientific evidence.

In the United States, Christianity plays a major role in history and public life. The first settlers were the so-called "Puritans" or "Pilgrim Fathers". They believed in the literal teachings of the Bible, and this was not welcome in England at the time. Having escaped religious persecution in Europe, they came to America to practise their religion freely. For them, America was the "New Jerusalem", a kind of spiritual promise of a new land or a kind of utopian society. Thus the "American Dream" has always had a strong religious side. We can still see this in many ways in modern America. The dollar bill states "In God we trust", there are many different kinds of Christian churches and practising a religion is much more common in the United States. Presidents and other politicians will frequently refer to God in their speeches and especially the Republican Party and the new movement of the Tea Party strongly emphasise Christian teachings. It is this kind of tradition that informs the Intelligent Design Movement. As a lot of people take a literal Christian belief for granted, there is a greater demand to include this view in schools. So they can count on a substantial group to support their ideas.

Notizen

Aufgabe 3

There should be no ethical limits to science. **Discuss.**

Lösungsschritte

1. Fertigen Sie zunächst eine Gliederung an. Zählen Sie positive und kritische Folgen der Wissenschaft auf, stellen Sie diese möglichst konkret dar. Denken Sie dabei einerseits an die Freiheit der Wissenschaft als Voraussetzung neuer Erkenntnisse, aber beziehen Sie auch Genforschung oder Atomenergie in Ihre Überlegungen ein.
2. Welche Gründe gibt es für die vorliegenden Haltungen?
3. Beziehen Sie sich auf die im Text genannten Haltungen gegenüber der Evolution und dem Unterricht in amerikanischen Schulen.
4. Formulieren Sie nun Ihren Text mit Einleitung (aktuelles Beispiel), Hauptteil und Schlussfolgerung. Äußern Sie Ihre Meinung zum Thema *Ethische Grenzen und freie Forschung*. Verbinden Sie Ihre Sätze mit Konnektoren.
5. Lesen Sie Ihren Text nochmals durch und korrigieren Sie Fehler.

Stichpunktlösung

- Possible arguments to support the statement: scientific research should not be hindered by traditional belief: if Galileo Galilei had been stopped successfully, we would still believe the earth was a disc; progress is not possible if there are limits; man can only develop if thought is free …,
- possible arguments against the statement: scientific research can lead to destruction; findings like how to build an atomic bomb are dangerous to mankind; scientists must be stopped if they do not feel responsible for their inventions; not everything that is possible is good, especially if it gets into the wrong hands; experiments on animals and human beings should not be allowed.

TRADITION AND CHANGE

Trainingsaufgabe 5

Aufgabentyp	Comprehension, analysis, evaluation
Thema	Globalisation – global challenges
Material	Tony Blair's Lord Mayor's Banquet Speech
Textsorte	Sach- und Gebrauchstext: Politische Rede
Niveau	Leistungskurs

Assignments

1. Outline Tony Blair's view of globalisation, the global challenges of our time and necessary political answers.

2. Explain how the Prime Minister uses argumentative structure, language and rhetorical devices to convince the audience of his view on globalisation

3. In lines 47–49 Tony Blair states: "In a modern world there is no security or prosperity at home unless we deal with the global challenges of conflict, terrorism, climate change and poverty. Self interest and mutual interest are inextricably linked. National interests can best be advanced through collective action." Comment on this statement and its implications for the richest countries and for yourself.

Material

Tony Blair's Lord Mayor's Banquet Speech

During a traditional dinner at the Guildhall in London on November 14, 2005, British Prime Minister Tony Blair made a major world affairs speech

Thirty years ago a political leader who said that the way to advance the national interest was through the spread, worldwide, of the values of democracy, justice and liberty, would have been called an idealist.
Today such a person is a realist. We describe the modern world as interdependent. We
5 acknowledge the force of globalisation. But we fail to follow through the logic of these realities in global politics.
Nations are deeply connected at every level. Of course, economically, but also now through communication, travel and technology.
Yesterday, by chance, I watched part of the MTV Music Awards. Well, it was certainly
10 the most relaxed part of the week I just had. I recommend it to any person who wants to understand modern politics. Why? There was no politics discussed. But the fusion of sounds, rhythms and musical influences from vastly different cultures was an allegory[1]

---

1 *here:* typical example

for today's world and the context in which politics exists. This is a world integrating at a fast rate, with enormous economic, cultural and political consequences.

And it all happens as a result of what people themselves are doing. Occasionally we debate globalisation as if it were something imposed by governments or business on unwilling people. Wrong. It is the individual decisions of millions of people that is creating and driving globalisation. Globalisation isn't something done to us. It is something we are, consciously or unconsciously, doing to and for ourselves.

[...]

... out of this great pumping up of global integration comes the need for stronger and more effective global, multilateral action. There is a real danger that the institutions of global politics lag seriously behind the challenges they are called upon to resolve.

These challenges are pressing. The most obvious is global terrorism. Barely a week goes by without another country being added to the grieving list of victims. Jordan, Egypt, Indonesia, India and of course here in London. Recently, in Australia, it appears an attack was foiled. We have disrupted two groups planning attacks here in the UK since 7 July alone. What is obvious now to all is that this is a global movement and requires global action in response, of which the successful completion of a democratic process in Afghanistan and Iraq is a major component. So is the push for peace between Israel and Palestine. In all of these conflicts, the only successful solution is based on democratic consent; and success would have a tremendous persuasive effect far beyond the frontiers of the countries concerned.

Similarly, with the challenge of climate change, the world has to act together. After Gleneagles[2] we began the G8 + 5[3] talks with the first meeting in London on November 1. The commitment period[4] under the Kyoto protocol[5] ends in 2012. We urgently need a framework, with the necessary targets, sensitively and intelligently applied over the right timeframe, that takes us beyond 2012.

It can only happen if the US, China and India join with Europe, Japan and others to create such a framework. Failure will mean not only increasing the damage to the environment but in a world of greater competition for carbon fuel, real pressure on energy supply and energy prices. Yet such an agreement cannot materialize without the major nations of the world agreeing an approach that is fair and balanced, sharing the most advanced science and technology to tackle carbon emissions. In other words, a just settlement as well as an effective one.

And we surely know already that if we leave millions of the world's poorest out of the onward march of global prosperity, we do not merely indicate moral indifference, but commit a foolish betrayal of our own long-term interest. [...]

In a modern world there is no security or prosperity at home unless we deal with the global challenges of conflict, terrorism, climate change and poverty. Self interest and mutual interest are inextricably linked. National interests can best be advanced through collective action.

Calculate not just the human misery of the poor themselves. Calculate our loss: the aid, the lost opportunity to trade, the short-term consequences of the multiple conflicts; the

---

2 a hotel in Scotland; *here:* the G8-summit in July, 2005, where the heads of government of Canada, France, Germany, Italy, Japan, Russia, the United Kingdom and the United States met to discuss international problems
3 G8 + 5 talks: the meeting of the eight politicians with the political leaders of Brazil, China, India, Mexico and South Africa
4 commitment period: a period of time for which plans and promises have been made
5 an international agreement from February 16, 2005 to reduce greenhouse gas emission worldwide

55 long-term consequences on the attitude to the wealthy world of injustice and abject deprivation amongst the poor. We will reap what we sow; live with what we do not act to change.
Here, in the City of London, which makes its living above all by being the meeting point of many nations, and which through trade creates much of the wealth on which this
60 British nation depends, is a good place for this call to action. So let us act.

(764 words)

Tony Blair's Lord Mayor's Banquet Speech, November 14, 2005, http://www.number-10.gov.uk/output/Page8524.asp

Lösungsvorschlag

Aufgabe 1

Outline Tony Blair's view of globalisation, the global challenges of our time and necessary political answers.

Lösungsschritte

1. Prüfen Sie die verwendeten Operatoren. Diese geben Ihnen genaue Informationen darüber, was Sie in der Aufgabe zu leisten haben (hier: *outline*).
2. Aktivieren Sie bereits vor dem ersten Lesen des Textes Ihr Hintergrundwissen und scannen Sie ihn dann gezielt nach Informationen zu den drei zu untersuchenden Aspekten. Markieren Sie diese entweder farbig im Text oder notieren Sie sie tabellarisch.
3. Unterstreichen Sie die wichtigen Fakten (keine Details, Beispiele, wörtliche Rede, Aufzählungen).
4. Benennen Sie Autor, Titel, Textart und Entstehungsjahr in Ihrem Einleitungssatz.
5. Lösen Sie sich vom Text und formulieren Sie eine kurze Zusammenfassung in eigenen Worten. Denken Sie an die Verwendung des Simple Present und von Konnektoren, damit die logischen Zusammenhänge deutlich werden.
6. Vermeiden Sie in diesem Aufgabenbereich Kommentare, persönliche Wertungen oder Analysen.
7. Beachten Sie, dass Sie weder wörtliche Rede noch Zitate verwenden dürfen.
8. Strukturieren Sie Ihren Text in *paragraphs*, welche jeweils nur einen Aspekt beinhalten sollten.

Stichpunktlösung

Globalisation:
- There is a global interdependence and networks are established among nations,
- the process of globalisation advances quickly and has dramatic consequences,
- people are taking part actively in this process and are thereby shaping their lives.

Global challenges of our time:
- There are a lot of global challenges, i.e. global conflicts and terrorism, climate change, poverty, competition for carbon fuel, which require rapid solutions.

Necessary political answers:
- According to Blair these global problems call for a framework that needs to be effective, feasible for a long period of time and therefore built upon a multilateral agreement,
- this framework is important because it serves personal interests like "prosperity" and "security",
- not having this kind of framework might effect a pressure on energy supplies and prices and further be a sign of moral indifference.

TRADITION AND CHANGE

Aufgabe 2

Explain how the Prime Minister uses argumentative structure, language and rhetorical devices to convince the audience of his view on globalisation.

Lösungsschritte

1. Prüfen Sie die verwendeten Operatoren. Diese geben Ihnen genaue Informationen darüber, was Sie in der Aufgabe zu leisten haben (hier: *explain*).
2. Analysieren Sie den Text in mehreren Schritten in Bezug auf die geforderten Teilbereiche (*argumentative structure*, *language* und *rhetorical devices*).
3. Rufen Sie sich für die Analyse der argumentativen Struktur Schlüsselbegriffe und typische Strukturelemente für political speeches ins Gedächtnis, z. B. *antithesis*, *sense units*.
4. Die Sprachanalyse (*language*) muss u. a. die Satzstruktur, die verwendete(n) Sprachebene(n), den Gebrauch von Zitaten und den Grad der Anschaulichkeit und Verständlichkeit der Sprache untersuchen.
5. Überlegen Sie, welche rhetorischen Figuren vermehrt in Reden vorkommen und welche Funktionen diese haben können.
6. Unterstreichen oder notieren Sie aussagekräftige Beispiele.
7. Formulieren Sie einen Einleitungssatz, in dem Sie sich auf die Aufgabenstellung beziehen.
8. Erläutern Sie immer auch die Funktion und Wirkung der von Ihnen analysierten Aspekte.
9. Strukturieren Sie Ihren Text in *paragraphs*, welche jeweils nur einen Aspekt beinhalten sollten.
10. Vergessen Sie nicht, am Ende eine zusammenfassende Schlussfolgerung zu formulieren.

Stichpunktlösung

Argumentative structure:

examples from the speech	effect
■ the text is divided into plausible sense units: introduction to the topic (historical development), description of globalisation and example, appeal/thesis, global challenges (examples and answers, self-interest and national interest in the topic, call to action)	■ clear structuring of the argumentation

examples from the speech	effect
■ the speaker makes use of antitheses/contrasts: "Thirty years ago ... Today ..."; "... something imposed by... Wrong."; "Globalisation isn't something done to us. It is something we are ... doing to and for ourselves."	■ pointing out developments or alternatives

Language:

examples from the speech	effect
■ the speech contains immediately understandable and well-known expressions like "march of global prosperity" ■ there is also a biblical quote: "We will reap what we sow." ■ the sentence structure is not very complex, there are even one-word sentences	■ easily understandable and vivid language
■ the speaker employs negatively connoted expressions: "moral indifference"; "a foolish betrayal" ■ negative consequences and unacceptable alternatives are described: "Failure will mean..."; "if we leave millions of the world's poorest out of ..."	■ the speaker's intention, i.e. to address the global challenges at hand, is presented as important and urgent

Rhetorical devices:

examples from the speech	effect
■ there are informal expressions ("well") ■ the speaker makes humorous remarks: "it was certainly the most relaxed part of the week ..." ■ the speaker uses an *inclusive* we ("we", "us", "our") ■ he also directly appeals to his audience: "Calculate ..."; "So let us act ..."	■ the speaker establishes a somewhat personal relationship, which makes the audience more prone to listen and agree to his arguments
■ **enumeration** of countries where there are victims of terrorism	■ the speaker uses this enumeration to stress the importance of his statement that the most obvious challenge is fighting terrorism

Notizen

examples from the speech	effect
■ **repetition (anaphora)**: "Calculate … Calculate …"	■ this makes a lasting impression on the audience; stressed in this way a statement is much easier to remember
■ a change of the regular sentence structure: *What is obvious* now to all is that …	■ this emphasizes that finally everybody has understood that these were no isolated incidents and that it is "a global movement which requires global action"
■ **adverbs** ("seriously"; "urgently") and **adjectives** ("pressing")	■ these also underline the importance of the speaker's deliberations, because the situation requires action

Aufgabe 3

In lines 47–49 Tony Blair states: "In a modern world there is no security or prosperity at home unless we deal with the global challenges of conflict, terrorism, climate change and poverty. Self interest and mutual interest are inextricably linked. National interests can best be advanced through collective action." **Comment** on this statement and its implications for the richest countries and for yourself.

HINWEIS Sie sollen das vorgestellte Zitat erläutern und aus zwei Perspektiven kommentieren. Zum einen sollen Sie die in Blairs Rede dargestellten Implikationen für die reichen (westlichen) Industrieländer aufzählen und kommentieren und zum anderen diejenigen, die sich für Sie persönlich ergeben.

Lösungsschritte

1. Prüfen Sie die verwendeten Operatoren. Diese geben Ihnen genaue Informationen darüber, was Sie in der Aufgabe zu leisten haben (hier: *comment on*).
2. Sammeln und erläutern Sie (tabellarisch oder in einer Mindmap) im Textauszug genannte oder angedeutete Konsequenzen von Blairs Forderung.
3. Ergänzen Sie zusätzlich Ihre eigenen Überlegungen. Achten Sie darauf, dass Sie systematisieren und dabei klar zwischen den zwei Anforderungsebenen (persönliche Implikationen, Implikationen für reiche Industrieländer) differenzieren.
4. Bringen Sie Ihre Ergebnisse in eine sinnvolle Reihenfolge. Gut ist hierbei, wenn Sie das jeweils beste Argument am Schluss benennen.
5. Formulieren Sie eine aussagekräftige These in der Einleitung Ihres Essays.
6. Vergessen Sie nicht, Ihre Thesen zu erläutern und durchgängig mit Beispielen zu veranschaulichen.
7. Denken Sie daran, eine zusammenfassende Schlussfolgerung zu formulieren.

Stichpunktlösung

- Blair's thesis that **national interests** require dealing with global challenges like conflict, terrorism, climate change and poverty is right insofar as all the apects he has mentioned influence everyone in the same way: national security is endangered by a global network of terrorism, therefore Britain has been assisting the US in the Iraq War; national prosperity is endangered by a limitation of external energy supplies or by constraints to free trade,
- one can easily find proposals for fighting these global challenges with **combined forces**: an example from the text is Blair's suggestion that there should be a follow-up agreement to the Kyoto protocol,
- another effect of combining forces could be that the UN's potential for action could be strengthened and broadened; besides, the G8 summit could and should become a powerful instrument for framing aims of mutual interest,
- still one must consider **different perspectives** from Blair's thesis:
  - on a personal level we all could do our daily share: for example fighting poverty by buying fair-trade products; we can also help save the climate by saving energy (e. g. using public transport more frequently, switching off electronic devices after use),
  - the implications for industrial nations go further: there would have to be contracts that ensure for example fair trade conditions or meeting environmental standards – both of which would have negative effects on short term cost-effectiveness; that means that there must be a compromise between the short-term financial interest of the nations and the global challenges which influence individual nations in the long run,
- one could also ask whether the common grounds which the wealthy nations share, e. g. the set of values like freedom, democracy and justice, are really dependably safe,
- one could argue that definitions of freedom and democracy are quite often influenced by economic interests; some argue that the USA's mission to bring freedom to Iraq has been strongly influenced by Iraq's possession of oil fields.

WORK AND INDUSTRIALISATION

Trainingsaufgabe 6

Aufgabentyp	Comprehension, analysis, evaluation (comment or re-creation of text: article)
Thema	Globalisation – global challenges
Material	Cynthia Tucker: *US Excess Vs. Nature's Limits*. In: *The Baltimore Sun*
Textsorte	Sachtext: Zeitungsartikel
Niveau	Grundkurs

Assignments

1. Point out the US use of resources and its global consequences according to the author's views.

2. Examine how Cynthia Tucker gains her readers' interest and convinces them that changes in their energy consumption are necessary. Consider aspects of content, composition and language.

3. Choose **one** of the following assignments:
   a) Considering the process of globalisation today, comment on Tucker's warning that "in the industrialized world […] we consume precious resources as if abundance were our birthright" (l. 11 f.).

   or

   b) According to Tucker, we are dependent on and addicted to oil (l. 27). Bearing in mind the environmental and personal implications at stake as presented in her text, write an article for your school magazine about the question if young people should own a car or not.

Material

Cynthia Tucker
US Excess Vs. Nature's Limits

The mythology of the Old West is replete with tales of dry land and drought, of parched landscapes and prayers for rain. Hollywood has told many a story of rainmakers – men, and occasionally women, who wandered the prairie with promises of a magic that could cause the heavens to open up and pour water down upon the earth.

5 Suddenly, the desperation that drove such claims doesn't seem so far-fetched in the Southeastern United States, where severe drought is drying up wells and emptying res-

ervoirs. Humanity has progressed mightily since the days of Conestoga wagons[1], but we still can't make rain.

Nor fossil fuels. Our technological breakthroughs are indeed miraculous, but mankind still cannot create one of the essentials of life – water – or one of the great luxuries of life: petroleum. There are limits.

Oddly, we seem to have hardly noticed. In the industrialized world, especially in the United States, we consume precious resources as if abundance were our birthright. And we're angered by anyone who suggests otherwise.

When President Jimmy Carter[2] was faced with an embargo by the Organization of Petroleum Exporting Countries, he responded by ordering conservation. Americans complied, but only grudgingly. And we despised him for insisting that we make do with less.

That's why no president has dared suggest since then that Americans make sacrifices, that we learn to live with limits. We want to drive Hummers[3] to work and plant rice in the desert. Somehow, the American Dream has become identified with excess: bigger houses, bigger cars, bigger bathrooms.

Meanwhile, fast-developing countries, especially India and China, admire our consumption patterns and copy our habits. They, too, want automobiles, air-conditioning, golf courses and shopping malls. Americans are hardly in a position to lecture them about conservation when we've set such a poor example.

So when the oil-rich sheikhs of the desert kingdom of Dubai build the world's biggest indoor ski resort, who are we to criticize? The sorry truth is that Americans are actually paying for that ski resort, and all the other fabulous excesses of Dubai, through our addiction to oil.

If there is any good news, it is this: We're becoming aware of the cost of our petroleum profligacy. Not only are we enriching jihadists[4] in oil-rich countries, but our consumption is also fueling climate change. The environmental agenda is gaining adherents. Besides, price tends to get our attention. With petroleum hovering near $100 a barrel, motorists are bound to use less. Congress may finally demand more fuel efficiency from automobiles and perhaps even get serious about investments in alternative fuels.

But a limited water supply is not something we've been forced to think about, especially in greener areas of the United States, like Georgia. We believe drought is cyclical. Many climatologists have warned, however, that one consequence of global warming is more frequent and more severe droughts. Maybe we should learn to live with fewer golf courses and swimming pools, with lawns that demand less pampering and cars that still look just fine with less washing.

We ought to set an example of conservation in a world with an expanding population and limited resources. Already, scientists predict that wars in the near future will be waged over water. Instead of modeling excess, perhaps the United States can be a model of temperance[5], of living within nature's bounds.

(563 words)

Cynthia Tucker: US Excess Vs. Nature's Limits. In: The Baltimore Sun, November 19, 2007

1 heavy horse-drawn wagons used during the westward expansion
2 President of the USA 1977–1981
3 brand of car that consumes a lot of petrol
4 fighter in a Muslim holy war
5 sensible control of the things you say and do

WORK AND INDUSTRIALISATION

Lösungsvorschlag

Aufgabe 1

Point out the US use of resources and its global consequences according to the author's views.

Lösungsschritte

1. Die Aufgabenstellung verstehen Sie, wenn Sie die Operatoren beachten.
2. Lesen Sie den Text noch einmal und markieren Sie wichtige Textstellen in der ersten Farbe. Die Leitfragen sind hierbei: Wie nutzen die USA ihre Ressourcen? Welche Konsequenzen hat dies in politischer und ökologischer Hinsicht?
3. Stellen Sie die Beschreibung in einer Stichpunktliste zusammen.
4. Strukturieren Sie den Text vor. Anschließend schreiben Sie ihn in eigenen Worten. Nennen Sie im Einleitungssatz die wesentlichen Daten der äußeren Textbeschreibung (z. B. Titel, Autor, Veröffentlichungsort und -datum). Achten Sie im Hauptteil darauf, dass Sie nicht analysieren, zitieren oder kommentieren!
5. Nehmen Sie abschließend eine Korrektur Ihrer typischen Fehler vor. (Dies machen Sie möglichst auch noch einmal ganz am Schluss der Klausur.)

Stichpunktlösung

Introductory sentence:
The newspaper article "US Excess Vs. Nature's Limits" by Cynthia Tucker, which was published in *The Baltimore Sun* on November 19, 2007, deals with the way Americans consume energy and its consequences for the world.

Resources are limited:
- Limited supply of fossil fuels
- Limited water supply
- Addiction to oil
- American profligacy of resources and the indignation of the people when asked to conserve energy (they want "bigger houses, bigger cars, bigger bathrooms")

Consequences:
- Developing countries (e. g. India and China) and petroleum exporting countries (e. g. Dubai) adapt to the consumer behavior of the American people
- Nearly impossible to ask these countries to behave ecologically correctly
- Extensive political and ecological consequences worldwide because of the uncontrolled profligacy and energy consumption (climate change, financing of jihads in petroleum exporting countries, drought)

LÖSUNG: TRAININGSAUFGABE 6

Aufgabe 2

Examine how Cynthia Tucker gains her readers' interest and convinces them that changes in their energy consumption are necessary. Consider aspects of content, composition and language.

Lösungsschritte

1. Die Aufgabenstellung verstehen Sie, wenn Sie die Operatoren beachten.
2. Lesen Sie den Text noch einmal und markieren Sie wichtige Textstellen in der zweiten Farbe. Die Leitfragen sind hierbei: Wie weckt die Autorin Interesse und wie überzeugt sie den Leser durch Inhalt, Aufbau des Textes und Sprache?
3. Stellen Sie die Erkenntnisse in einer Stichpunktliste in zwei Spalten zusammen – linke Spalte: Zitate/Textstellen, rechte Spalte: eigene Kommentare, Erklärungen.
4. Strukturieren Sie den Text anhand der Stichpunktliste vor und schreiben Sie ihn anschließend:
   - Einleitung (kurz den Bezug zur Aufgabenstellung herstellen)
   - Hauptteil (Nennung der relevanten Textstellen sowie inhaltlich relevanter Aspekte und Erklärung der jeweiligen Funktion im Hinblick auf die Leitfragen)
   - Schluss (kurze Zusammenfassung der wichtigsten Ergebnisse der Analyse in einem Satz)

   Achten Sie darauf, dass analysespezifisch gearbeitet wird. Zitate benutzen Sie als Belege. Denken Sie daran, keine eigene Meinung zu äußern.
5. Überprüfen Sie die eigene Analyse noch einmal daraufhin, ob der Bezug zur Leitfrage in allen Punkten vorhanden ist, d. h. sich wie ein roter Faden durch die Analyse zieht.
6. Nehmen Sie abschließend eine Korrektur Ihrer typischen Fehler vor.
   (Dies machen Sie möglichst auch noch einmal ganz am Schluss der Klausur.)

Stichpunktlösung

Introduction:
The author wants Americans to change their consumer behavior. This is important because America's standards are often copied by the rest of the world. To gain the reader's attention the author makes use of several devices.

Main part:

Argumentative structure	Author refers to history	- "Old West" ("dry land" (l. 1), "Conestoga wagons" (l. 7)
	Author refers to current problems (e. g. oil price shock)	- "petroleum hovering near $100 a barrel" (l. 34)
	Author has a threatening forecast for the future (e. g. droughts)	- "We believe drought is cyclical." (l. 38)

WORK AND INDUSTRIALISATION

	Author appeals to readers to change their behaviour	■ "Maybe we should learn to live with fewer golf courses …" (ll. 40–42) ■ "We ought to set an example …" (ll. 43–44)	
■ Rhetorical devices	Author stimulates interest and underlines urgency by making use of: ■ enumeration	■ "bigger houses, bigger cars, bigger bathrooms" (ll. 21–22) ■ "They, too, want automobiles, air-conditioning, golf courses and shopping malls." (ll. 24–25) ■ "with fewer golf courses and swimming pools, with lawns …" (ll. 40–41)	
	■ repetition	■ "bigger houses, bigger cars, bigger bathrooms" (ll. 21–22)	
	■ alliteration	■ "dry land and drought" (l. 1) ■ "waged over water" (l. 45)	
	■ rhetorical question	■ "[…] who are we to criticize?" (l. 28)	
	■ antithesis	■ "Our technological breakthroughs are indeed miraculous, but mankind still cannot create one of the essentials of life – water – or …" (ll. 9–10) ■ "expanding population and limited resources" (ll. 43–44)	
	■ metaphors	■ "[…] could cause the heavens to open up and pour water down […]" (l. 4) ■ "fueling climate change" (l. 33)	

Notizen

Content: criticism	Author criticizes Americans for thinking that the American Dream can only be achieved through excessive energy consumption	■ "We want to drive Hummers to work" (l. 20) ■ "[we want to] plant rice in the desert" (ll. 20–21) ■ "bigger houses, bigger cars, bigger bathrooms" (ll. 21–22)
Direct address of the reader	Author tries to convince readers of her position/author wants readers to think about their energy consumption by: ■ use of pronouns ■ examples ■ word fields	 ■ collective we (e.g. "our", "we") ■ "Maybe we should learn to live with fewer golf courses ..." (ll. 40–41) ■ (e.g.) "drought", "abundance"

Aufgabe 3 a

Considering the process of globalisation today, **comment** on Tucker's warning that "in the industrialized world [...] we consume precious resources as if abundance were our birthright" (l. 11 f.).

HINWEIS   Der *comment* soll sich mit der Aussage Tuckers beschäftigen, dass in der industrialisierten Welt kostbare Ressourcen verschwendet würden, so als ob dies ein Geburtsrecht wäre. Nach einer kurzen Erörterung des Zitats müssen Sie sowohl Argumente des Ausgangstextes als auch Ihnen bekannte aktuelle Debatten zum Thema einbeziehen. Schließlich müssen Sie selbst Position zum Textzitat beziehen.

Lösungsschritte

1. Die Aufgabenstellung verstehen Sie, wenn Sie die Operatoren beachten.
2. Lesen Sie den Text noch einmal und markieren Sie wichtige Textstellen in der dritten Farbe. Leitfrage hierbei: Welche Position bezieht die Autorin in ihrem Artikel?
3. Brainstorming:
    ■ Finden Sie Argumente im Ausgangstext, die Sie weiter ausführen können.
    ■ Finden Sie Aspekte der aktuellen Umweltdebatte.
    ■ Erklären Sie Ihre Position zum Thema.
    (Sie können dies als Mindmap oder auch in Listenform aufschreiben.)
4. Strukturieren Sie den Text, nachdem Sie Ihre Stichpunkte sortiert haben:
    ■ Einleitung (das Zitat und seine Bedeutung)
    ■ Hauptteil (Argumente im Text/die aktuelle Umweltdebatte/die eigene Position)
    ■ überzeugendes Fazit

5. Sammeln Sie satz- und textverbindende Wörter/Mittel (*connectives and conjunctions*).
6. Schreiben Sie den Text.
7. Lesen Sie Ihren Text abschließend: Ist der Text sinnvoll und logisch aufgebaut? Sind die einzelnen Punkte gut verknüpft? Überzeugen Sie Ihren Leser?
8. Nehmen Sie abschließend eine Korrektur Ihrer typischen Fehler vor.
(Dies machen Sie möglichst auch noch einmal ganz am Schluss der Klausur.)

Stichpunktlösung

The quote:
Cynthia Tucker claims that people in the industrialized world consume precious resources as if abundance is their birthright. She points out that:
- profligacy increased in the course of industrialization,
- the energy crisis of the 21st century is an obvious result of the profligacy of resources,
- Americans think that they have the right to waste precious resources, which makes them look arrogant.

Arguments in the article:
- The author is right when she claims that Americans have to change their patterns of consumption. They do not care a lot about energy consumption and nobody dares to tell them to make any concessions.
- Americans criticized President Carter when he ordered conservation (cf. ll. 15–18).
- No president has dared suggest that Americans make sacrifices ever since (cf. l. 19).
- America's status as a role model for up-and-coming industrial nations (cf. ll. 23–26).

Current events:
- The Kyoto Protocol: important nations such as the United States did not ratify it.
- Al Gore as former Vice President of the United States appeals to the public with speeches and the documentary movie An Inconvenient Truth. He wants Americans and people all over the world to think about climate change and what each one of us can do about it.
- Personal implications and aspects of the effects of global warming (e.g. disappearance of the ice caps, higher energy costs, droughts, floods, mega-fires)

Own position:
- Cynthia Tucker's warning is justified.
- The author's ideas cannot be put into practice without a long-term environmental policy.
- The interests of developing countries should be borne in mind.

Aufgabe 3 b

According to Tucker, we are dependent on and addicted to oil (l. 30). Bearing in mind the environmental and personal implications at stake as presented in her text, **write** an article for your school magazine about the question if young people should own a car or not.

Lösungsschritte

1. Die Aufgabenstellung verstehen Sie, wenn Sie die Operatoren beachten.
2. Lesen Sie den Text noch einmal und markieren Sie wichtige Textstellen in der dritten Farbe. Leitfrage hierbei: Inwiefern zeigt sich, dass wir von Öl abhängig sind?
3. Brainstorming (z. B. als Mindmap):
   - Problemstellung
   - Vergleich der eigenen Situation mit der im Artikel dargestellten
   - Argumente für ein eigenes Auto
   - Argumente gegen ein eigenes Auto
   - Fazit: persönliche Meinung
4. Sortieren Sie die Stichpunkte und strukturieren Sie den Text.
5. Schreiben Sie den Artikel unter Berücksichtigung der Leserlenkung. (Benutzen Sie sprachliche Mittel für einen argumentativen Text in einer Zeitung.)
6. Lesen Sie Ihren Text abschließend: Ist der Text sinnvoll und logisch aufgebaut? Sind die einzelnen Punkte gut verknüpft?
7. Finden Sie eine mitreißende Überschrift.
8. Nehmen Sie abschließend eine Korrektur Ihrer typischen Fehler vor. (Dies machen Sie möglichst auch noch einmal ganz am Schluss der Klausur.)

Ausführliche Lösung

We can make a change

Melting ice caps, droughts in Africa, the Americas, Europe, floods in England and Germany, mega-fires in Australia, California and Southern Europe. What do these have to do with us? All these environmental problems all over the world cannot be the result of the consumer behaviour of teenagers here in Germany. Scaremongering, most of us say. But are these really just scare stories?

Students in our school love the luxurious life. We love indoor skiing in summer, taking long showers as often as twice a day, lots of multimedia devices in our rooms and much more. We waste energy every day without even realizing it. And we love to drive our own cars.

A car means freedom. With your own car you do not have to depend on your parents or public transport any longer. It does not matter where you want to go: your car will take you there. No longer will you have to change buses a couple of times before arriving at your destination. No longer will you have to ask your parents to drive you to the other end of town. You are absolutely independent from the schedules of public transport. Who does not know the feeling of standing at a bus stop waiting for a bus? Especially on rainy days or in winter this is often unpleasant. Furthermore we students know what it means to stand in crowded buses hoping to reach the exit when we approach our destination. With your own car you always have a seat. You can also bring all the bags and non-essential items you otherwise would consider leaving at home because you do not want to carry them all the way to school. Other students respect you more than they would if you did not have a car. You can be part of the class when you offer others a ride home. For students who live in rural areas a car is a blessing. Finally they do not have to get up at 4.30 in the morning to arrive at school in time.

But on the other hand is it worth having a car of your own when we think about the consequences for our environment? We pollute the air we breathe with our exhaust fumes just to have a convenient life. More and more cars block up the streets and we need more time to get to our destinations. More cars mean more pollution. And more cars mean that we need more and more gasoline to get from one place to another. This leads to increasing gasoline prices because precious resources are being used up slowly but surely. For many of us the question whether we really need a car never comes up. Having a driver's license means owning a car as soon as possible.

All in all we waste oil although we could live without cars of our own. We use cars without thinking about the consequences for our future life, the consequences for our Earth. Certainly some of us really need a car, for example the students living in rural areas. But do we really all have to come to school in our own cars? Why do we not go on using the bus as we have been doing for years? Just because we are too lazy and comfort-loving? Why do we not at least have carpools? This would mean less searching for a spot to park the car, less traffic on the roads and, most importantly, fewer wasted resources. Because we are responsible for the melting ice caps, the droughts, the floods, the megafires. We can make a change. We can save our planet. But we have to start now. As long as emission-free cars are not available and our cars waste gasoline as well as money, we should be responsible and go by bus, ride bikes or walk as we did before turning eighteen.

(653 words)

Notizen

EXTREME SITUATIONS

Trainingsaufgabe 7

Aufgabentyp	Description, analysis, discussion
Thema	Extreme situations
Material	Stephen Amidon: *Human Capital* (Auszug)
Textsorte	Romanauszug
Niveau	Leistungskurs

Assignments

1. Briefly outline the situation and describe how Shannon and Ian respond to it.
2. Analyse their moral conflict and compare it to a similarly difficult situation encountered in a text read in class.
3. Discuss whether choice or chance plays a more important role in modern man's life.

Material

Stephen Amidon
Human Capital

Shannon and Jamie are high school seniors; Ian has dropped out of school and now works in a deli. As Shannon's boyfriend Jamie kept getting drunk, she left him. One night, however, she is called to a party because Jamie has had too much to drink.
She and Ian, her new boyfriend, go there. Shannon drives Jamie home while Ian takes Jamie's Jeep Wrangler back and hits a cyclist. Shannon picks Ian up at Jamie's house. On the way to Ian's place, they see bystanders attending to the victim of the accident.

"Look, Shannon, it was an accident, all right? The car just – I was downshifting, and when I hit the gas, I mean, it just lurched away from me. It was like a rocket taking off. And the next thing I knew this guy appeared out of the middle of nowhere."
"I know it was an accident."
5 "Then what possible reason would there be for me to get myself arrested? If he was still lying out there or they needed my blood or something ... he's not going to get any better with us calling the cops. I get busted[1] and that's it for me."
He folded his arms across his chest and bent forward slightly. Shannon put her hand on her back and could feel his body shaking. Headlights appeared on Totten Pike. They
10 watched through the picture window as a car drove by without slowing.
"We'll wait until morning," she said.
He put his head back on her lap. She began to stroke his hair.
"Hey, Ian?" she asked after a while, "How come you drove the Jeep all the way back to

---
1 to get arrested

Jamie's?"

"I thought it would be easier."

"But what happened on the hill?" she asked softly.

"I don't know. I wasn't even going that fast. It just … the car just sort of jumped. It was like the thing was driving itself. I thought …"

"What?"

"I don't know what I thought."

He began to cry, a rhythmic stutter of his breathing, his hand gripping her knee. She thought he was shivering at first. She'd never seen him cry before. After a minute of this she felt something hot soak through the fabric on her thigh. Tears. He stopped after that. He was so still that she thought he'd fallen asleep. She slid out from under him, getting one of Ginny's misshapen handmade quilts from the closet to put over his body. But when she came back to the sofa, she saw that his eyes were wide open. There was nothing behind them. They were all pure brilliant surface.

"I thought you were asleep."

"I don't think I'm ever going to sleep again."

She covered him, and then they watched the television with the sound turned off, a Hartford station, evangelists and infomercials, a guy with big rubber gloves cutting up baked chickens. […]

Finally, just as light was beginning to leak through the trees across the highway, the local morning news broadcast started. They turned on the sound. The story came on a good ten minutes into the program. […] The newscaster explained that the police were appealing for witnesses in a hit-and-run accident involving a Totten Crossing man named Robert Jarvis, who was in serious condition at Mercy Hospital. The whole thing took no more than thirty seconds of airtime.

"Serious," Shannon said. "What does that mean?"

"It means he's alive."

She knew it meant more than that but kept quiet. They watched the news on another station, but there was nothing there. Shannon turned off the television.

"So what are we going to do?" she asked.

"Nothing."

"Ian, we can't just do nothing."

He looked out the picture window at the rocky yard. She put her hand on the back of his neck. The muscles were rigid.

"Okay," he said, taking a deep breath. "If he's hurt badly, I mean, you know, really serious, then I'll turn myself in. But if he's just, if he's going to get better, then I won't. That's – that's all right, isn't it?"

Shannon nodded, even though she knew it wasn't all right. And then she thought of something else.

"But what if they figure out it was the Wrangler?"

"Okay. That, too. If they start asking about the Wrangler, we'll call them."

They went to his room and lay on top of the covers, keeping their clothes on. They didn't say anything, and Shannon must have drifted off, because the next thing she knew it was very bright in the room, a harsh, headachy light that seemed to be coming from a closer sun. Ian was sitting at his desk, drawing furiously in one of his pads[2]. He hadn't slept. He hadn't been anywhere near sleep.

"What time is it?" she asked.

---

2 writing/drawing pad

He closed the pad and looked at her.

"Late morning. Everything's cool."

"I'd better go," she said. "See what's happening."

He nodded unhappily.

"Call me."

"Ian, I'm not going to let you go through anything alone."

"And you won't tell anyone unless we decide together, right?"

"Ian, I promise."

They kissed for a while, and she allowed herself to believe everything was going to be all right. But once she was away from him, the magnitude of what they were doing returned. Keeping the accident a secret had seemed possible when she was lying with him in the quiet house, the world nothing more than passing traffic. But as she drove back into Totten Crossing, moving among all the regular people doing regular things, parents spending money and taking their kids places, she knew this was just an illusion.

(844 words)

Stephen Amidon, Human Capital, New York (Viking), 2004, S. 190–193

LÖSUNG: TRAININGSAUFGABE 7

Lösungsvorschlag

Aufgabe 1

Briefly **outline** the situation and **describe** how Shannon and Ian respond to it.

Lösungsschritte

1. Markieren Sie im Text die relevanten Informationen (Umstände des Unfalls, Reaktion der beiden Protagonisten).
2. Formulieren Sie Ihre Antwort sorgfältig, übernehmen Sie keine Passagen aus der Vorlage.
3. Korrigieren Sie Ihre Fehler.

Stichpunktlösung

- Shannon is called to fetch former boyfriend, Jamie, from a party – he is drunk,
- Ian, Shannon's new boyfriend, accompanies her,
- Shannon takes Jamie back to his place while Ian drives Jamie's jeep home,
- on his way back Ian hits a cyclist but leaves the scene of the accident,
- at home: Ian tells Shannon about the accident – he sees no reason to report the incident to the police,
- Ian deeply affected emotionally: trembles, cries, thinks he will never sleep again,
- Shannon comforts him, stays with him,
- after watching local news, Shannon and Ian discuss how they can solve the situation,
- if cyclist is seriously injured or if police ask about jeep, Ian agrees to give himself up,
- Shannon tries to persuade herself everything might turn out all right – realises in reality this solution is only an illusion.

Aufgabe 2

Analyse their moral conflict and **compare** it to a similarly difficult situation encountered in a text read in class.

Lösungsschritte

1. Ausgehend von der Beschreibung der Reaktionen in Aufgabe 1 müssen Sie nun den Konflikt analysieren.
2. Stellen Sie Shannons und Ians Werte bzw. die Werte der amerikanischen Gesellschaft einerseits (Hilfsbereitschaft, Loyalität) und ihre Reaktionen auf den Unfall andererseits gegenüber.
3. Beziehen Sie sich nun auf Texte aus dem Unterricht (z.B. die Unfallszene in *The Tortilla Curtain*, Winstons Reaktion im Verhör in *1984*, Hamlets Zweifel, ob er den Mord an seinem Vater rächen darf). Gehen Sie möglichst genau auf die Unterrichtstexte ein und beziehen Sie diese explizit auf den Klausurtext. Verbinden Sie Ihre Gedanken durch Konnektoren (z.B. *while*, *whereas*, *when*).
4. Lesen Sie Ihren Text nochmals kritisch durch und verbessern Sie Fehler.

Stichpunktlösung

- Ian/Shannon in an extreme dilemma – forced to test their moral/social standards against the fact of Ian's situation, i.e. having caused injury through momentary inattention.
- Ian, as Shannon's new boyfriend, cares for her and accompanies her to fetch her former boyfriend, who she still feels responsible for,
- Ian takes Jamie's car home so that nobody steals it; Jamie has no further inconvenience,
- contrast: image of helpful American teenager – causes a serious hit-and-run accident,
- confusion: no firm internal pattern of action – theoretical moral values vanish as Ian returns to childish behaviour: runs away, hides, pretends nothing serious has happened (ll. 23–32),
- compensates by pursuing other (drawing) activities (ll. 58–61),
- conflict: might be arrested – no trust in police as school dropout who might be expected to cause trouble – knows that once he is in prison his life is over,
- will only turn himself in if victim seriously injured or police find out about car,
- although aware of consequences, ruthless enough to allow others to suffer for his actions.
- Shannon feels responsible for Jamie, who has an alcohol problem and does not care about his health,
- now Ian might be prosecuted she cares for him: comforts him/tries to believe his story (ll. 8–9),
- she knows the consequences of hit-and-run accidents – tries to persuade Ian to turn himself in (ll. 45, 48–54),
- torn between love for Ian and her moral code (l. 51) – furthermore, knows Ian's solution is unrealistic, will have to face truth soon (ll. 72–75) – have to sacrifice themselves to their moral principles to help a totally immoral person (Jamie).
- *The Tortilla Curtain*: Delaney in similar situation: caused car accident and injured a man,
- contrast: initially Delaney shows more maturity: stops/cares for victim – on learning that he is an illegal immigrant, compassion turns into anger – blames the victim for being there,
- change shows Delaney (like Ian) is trying to rid himself of guilt feelings by abandoning his moral code (reduces Mexican to his ethnic origin/illegal presence),
- conflict: Delaney recognises xenophobia/racism of social class – no wish to support racism, but fears social exclusion if he helps Mexican victim,
- in both texts, protagonists in a tragic moral dilemma: their own needs/moral code against the bare reality that perverts them,
- both faced with decision involving inevitable personal sacrifice.

Aufgabe 3

Discuss whether choice or chance plays a more important role in modern man's life.

Lösungsschritte

1. Machen Sie sich Notizen zum Thema. Welche Beispiele/Texte unterstützen die Thesen der *choice*, welche Beispiele können Sie für *chance* heranziehen? Sie können sich auf gesellschaftliche oder politische Zusammenhänge beziehen (z. B. Arbeitsbedingungen, Globalisierung, Migration usw. als bestimmende Faktoren im Leben. Ebenso ist es denkbar, sich auf fiktionale Texte zu beziehen. Für *choice* z. B. *American Dream* (*hard work leads to success in The Pursuit of Happyness*) für *chance* z. B. *Forrest Gump*. *Macbeth* liefert Ansätze für beide Interpretationen.
2. Strukturieren Sie Ihre Gedanken, bevor Sie mit der Antwort beginnen.
3. Denken Sie daran, eine kurze Einleitung zu formulieren.
4. Stellen Sie dann beide Aspekte – *choice* und *chance* – dar und belegen Sie Ihre Thesen durch vielfältige Beispiele.
5. Beenden Sie den Text mit einer Stellungnahme. In diesem Fall können Sie auch differenzieren, z. B. je besser die ökonomischen und politischen Rahmenbedingungen, desto mehr hat das Individuum die Möglichkeit, das Schicksal aktiv zu bestimmen.
6. Achten Sie beim erneuten Lesen auf Fehler.

Stichpunktlösung

- Individual life moulded by many factors: social environment, family situation, economic status, education, development of personal talents/abilities: little room for chance?
- Political/economic developments incl. globalisation offer people both more choice and more restrictions.

More choice

- Traditional learning techniques no longer apply: new skills needed in shorter time due to pace of technological development – chance to develop new abilities,
- choice of studying abroad, contacting new people/culture, maybe finding future occupation,
- constant change in global markets leads to demand for fresh approach to vocational training – result: creation of new jobs/professions as substitute for traditional ones – not only one, but several jobs, have to be learnt in a person's working life,
- increasing political stabilisation through economic development – e. g. growth of GDP in South Africa – more choice for individual people – result: more opportunities for the individual.

More restrictions

- Opening up of world markets – low-paid labour preferred – industries outsource to low-wage economies – result: higher unemployment in developed/traditional regions,
- economic migration affects family life (single-person households, one-/absent-parent families etc.),

- result: development in some regions, extinction in others, (creation/death of communities) – physical/psychological effects on human beings,
- political development, e.g. wars, affects global (political, economic) development,
- modern man: more choice than in previous times due to fast development in all fields,
- chance plays a decisive role – many inventions unthinkable without random choice (software development/Bill Gates, genetic engineering),
- film example *Forrest Gump*: protagonist did not choose his life, it developed by chance – expresses human hope that chance makes life a fascinating adventure, no matter how carefully a person may plan/structure his or her life – chance/random choice gives people the opportunity to grow, develop and reach new heights.

Notizen

THE DYNAMICS OF CHANGE

Trainingsaufgabe 8

Aufgabentyp	Comprehension, interpretation, discussion
Thema	Canadian Literature, Science and Technology
Material	Margaret Atwood: *Oryx and Crake* Margaret Atwood: *Survival*
Textsorte	Romanauszug und Sachtext
Niveau	Grundkurs und Leistungskurs

Assignments

1. Describe the 'Crakers'.
2. Interpret the text *Oryx and Crake* in view of Atwood's theory of survival.
3. Discuss the opportunities and dangers of the genetic engineering of plants, animals or humans.

Material 1

Margaret Atwood
Oryx and Crake

Crake is a talented scientist in the near future. Jimmy, his old school friend, is visiting him in 'Paradice' (= the secret research unit at RejoovenEsense - a huge corporation specialised on a new secret genetic development). In this extract, Crake is going to show Jimmy his life's work.

Crake led Jimmy along and around; then they were standing in front of a large picture window. No: a one way mirror. Jimmy looked in. There was a large central space filled with trees, above them a blue sky. (Not really a blue sky, only the curved ceiling of the bubble-dome, with a clever projection device that simulated dawn, sunlight, evening,
5 night.) [...]
That was his first view of the Crakers. They were naked [...] At first he couldn't believe them, they were so beautiful. Black, yellow, white, brown, all available skin colours. [...]
"At first," said Crake, "we had to alter ordinary human embryos, which we got from - never mind where we got them. But these people are reproducing themselves now.
10 Also they're programmed to drop dead at age thirty - suddenly without getting sick. No old age, none of those anxieties."

Crake goes on to explain to Jimmy, that the results of his research are totally secret at the moment.

"Until we go public," said Crake. Very soon, RejoovenEsense hoped to hit the market.
15 They'd be able to create totally chosen babies that would incorporate any feature, physical, mental or spiritual, that the buyer might wish to select. [...]

It was amazing – said Crake – what once unimaginable things had been accomplished by the team here. What had been altered was the human brain. Gone were its destructive features, the features responsible for the world's current illnesses. For instance –
20 racism had been eliminated in the model group: the Paradice people simply did not register skin colour. Hierarchy could not exist among them, they lacked the neural complexes that would have created it. As they were neither hunters nor farmers, they were not hungry for land. They ate nothing but leaves and grass and roots and a berry or two; thus their foods were always plentiful and always available. [...]
25 As there would never be anything for these people to inherit, there would be no family trees, no marriages, and no divorces. They were perfectly adjusted to their habitat, so they would never have to create houses or tools or weapons, or clothing. They would have no need to invent harmful symbolisms, such as kingdoms, icons, gods or money. [...]

Soon after this, Crake destroys all human life (with the exception of Jimmy) by a virus he has created. He allows Jimmy to shoot him and Jimmy becomes the mentor of the Crakers, who now leave the laboratory and settle in the outside world.

(463 Words)

Margaret Atwood: Oryx and Crake, New York: Anchor Books, 2003, pp. 363–367

Material 2

Margaret Atwood
Survival

I'd like to begin with a sweeping generalization and argue that every country or culture has a single unifying and informing symbol at its core. [...] Possibly the symbol for America is The Frontier, a flexible idea that contains many elements dear to the American heart: it suggests a place that is new, where the old order can be discarded [...]; a
5 line that is always expanding, taking in or "conquering" ever-fresh virgin territory [...]; it holds out a hope, never fulfilled but always promised, of Utopia, the perfect human society. [...]
The central symbol for Canada [...] is undoubtedly Survival, la Survivance. [...] For early explorers and settlers, it meant bare survival in the face of "hostile" elements and/or
10 natives: carving out a place and a way of keeping alive. But the word can also suggest survival of a crisis or disaster, like a hurricane or a wreck, and many Canadian poems have this kind of survival as a theme; what you might call 'grim' survival as opposed to 'bare' survival. [...] But the main idea is the first one: hanging on, staying alive. [...]

(185 words)

Excerpt from Survival, by Margaret Atwood. Originally published by McClelland & Stewart, 1972. Copyright Margaret Atwood. Reprinted with permission of the author.

THE DYNAMICS OF CHANGE

Lösungsvorschlag

Aufgabe 1

Describe the 'Crakers'.

HINWEIS Markieren Sie im Text alle relevanten Stellen und beschreiben Sie die Merkmale der neuen Rasse möglichst genau. Achten Sie darauf, keine Textpassagen aus dem Originaltext zu übernehmen, und verwenden Sie Konjunktionen, um Zusammenhänge logisch deutlich zu machen.

Lösungsschritte

1. Beschreiben Sie das Aussehen und die Lebenswelt der künstlichen Wesen.
2. Gehen Sie nun kurz auf Gewohnheiten und das soziale Umfeld (Ernährung, Alters- und Sozialstruktur, fehlende Hierarchien, kein Rassismus) und die daraus resultierenden Verhaltensweisen ein (kein Territorialanspruch, keine aggressive Verteidigung von Lebensraum).
3. Schließlich ist noch auf spiritueller Ebene die fehlende Religiosität zu nennen.
4. Verfassen Sie nun Ihren Text.
5. Korrigieren Sie Fehler.

Stichpunktlösung

- 'Crakers' = Crake's creation = new race by genetic engineering/by changing human embryos,
- they reproduce themselves,
- artificial world/under a dome which simulates the times of the day inside the laboratory,
- beautiful and naked,
- all skin colours = blind to the difference of skin colours = consequence: no racism,
- die at 30 = no old age and no problems and worries connected with growing old,
- company RejoovenEsense wants to sell them to parents, who can choose the baby's looks and its character traits,
- no hierarchy,
- eat only leaves, grass and roots = no need to fight for land,
- no need for houses or clothes = adapted to their surroundings,
- no need for tools or weapons = they do not defend anything,
- no material possessions and no family structure,
- no need for God/religion.

Aufgabe 2

Interpret the text *Oryx and Crake* in view of Atwood's theory of survival.

HINWEIS Achten Sie bei dieser Aufgabe darauf, zunächst die Theorie des Überlebens als Leitmotiv der kanadischen Literatur in eigenen Worten darzustellen. Zeigen Sie dann Parallelen und Unterschiede zum vorliegenden Text auf. Zitieren Sie die Texte, um Ihre Thesen zu untermauern.

Lösungsschritte

1. Stellen Sie zunächst die Theorie des *Survival* dar.
2. Gehen Sie dann auf Gemeinsamkeiten mit dem vorliegenden Text ein (Außenwelt: Jimmy und Crake; Innenwelt: Neue Rasse kann mit minimaler Nahrung und ohne Kleidung überleben, ist gut an Umwelt angepasst).
3. Zeigen Sie im Anschluss Unterschiede auf.
4. Sie können am Ende eine Schlussfolgerung wagen, ob die Theorie auch in diesem Text zum Tragen kommt.
5. Verbessern Sie beim erneuten Lesen Fehler.

Stichpunktlösung

Introduction:
- Atwood argues that all Canadian literature is based on the idea of 'survival' and she explains which forms this survival can take: the 'bare survival' of the first settlers when faced with a threatening environment, and the 'grim survival' after a natural disaster or a disease.
- This novel has two societies: the outside world, where Jimmy and Crake live, and the inside world of the Crakers. Later the Crakers will go and live in the outside world.

Outside world (Jimmy and Crake):
- Crake interferes with human life by using genetic engineering on embryos, he has no scruples about intervening with a human embryo, the embryo is 'killed' to create a new form of life (a balance of survival and death),
- he has also created a disease which kills most people on earth (no survival),
- he does not seem to like the human race as it is,
- his science puts a stop to human survival, humans are doomed to die,
- for reasons unknown, Crake allows his friend Jimmy to kill him (no survival intended),
- maybe he is not happy with the consequences of what he has done / he feels guilty about what he has done,
- maybe Crake does not want to live in a world ruled by science and powerful corporations,
- Jimmy will be the (seemingly only) survivor of the lethal disease. There is one survivor and many deaths ('grim survival'),
- he will be a mentor for the Crakers (new start, give a new form of life a chance).

Inside world (Crakers):
- Crakers = Crake's dream race,
- he seems to be very proud of them ("It was amazing – said Crake – what once unimaginable things had been accomplished by the team here.", ll. 17–18),
- this race is supposed to survive the catastrophe and start a new perfect kind of society,
- destructive racism: eliminated in new race ("Gone were its destructive features [...] racism had been eliminated in the model group.", ll. 18–20),
- destructive hierarchies lead to wars = Crakers are immune to them ("Hierarchies could not exist among them.", l. 21),

- Crakers do not have possessions (no materialism),
- Crakers lead totally sustainable lifestyles, they only consume a minimum and do not destroy nature,
- they are well adapted to their environment and able to survive ("They ate nothing but leaves and grass and roots and a berry or two; thus their foods were always plentiful and always available.", ll. 23–24),
- his creation overcomes all negative trends in the outside world that Crake lives in,
- however, they are programmed to die at the age of 30 to avoid the painful process of ageing and dying slowly,
- they are unable to struggle for survival, it is not an option,
- utopian element: a new society with perfectly adapted creatures. Similarities to *Brave New World* (Alphas, Betas …), in both books a superior intelligence creates them, eliminating features that may harm them or the stability of society.

Conclusion:
- The Crakers seem to be positive beings, who are more peaceful and better than the human race, lacking all its destructive features. However, they are also doomed to death. Yet, their death is totally natural and peaceful. It excludes tragedy as they have no idea of a 'struggle for survival'. They take life for granted and death is part of it. The idea seems utopian and perfect. However, they lack deeper human feelings like love or family relations. One asks oneself, what do they live for?
- In the outside world, impending doom in the form of Crake's artificial lethal disease looms over mankind. Crake, too, is prepared to die (even though we are left to guess at his reasons). He has destined Jimmy to be the sole survivor of this catastrophe. Here the concepts of death and survival play a major role.

Aufgabe 3

Discuss the opportunities and dangers of the genetic engineering of plants, animals or humans.

HINWEIS Stellen Sie Vor- und Nachteile der Gentechnik dar, arbeiten Sie möglichst konkret mit Beispielen, um Ihre Behauptungen zu belegen. Sie können auch hier Bezüge zum vorliegenden Text herstellen.

Lösungsschritte

1. Sammeln Sie einige Punkte für die kurze Einleitung, hier können Sie Kenntnisse über den Forschungsstand in den Biowissenschaften einbringen.
2. Stellen Sie Vor- und Nachteile der Genforschung gegenüber und führen Sie möglichst konkrete Beispiele an.
3. Wägen Sie Pro und Kontra ab und kommen Sie zu einer begründeten Schlussfolgerung. Sie kann kritisch sein und auf die Unsicherheiten der neuen Technologie verweisen oder die Vision einer positiven Zukunft herstellen.
4. Verbessern Sie beim erneuten Lesen Fehler.

Stichpunktlösung

Introduction:
- Genetic manipulation of embryos to create a new race is science fiction.
- But part of this is reality, e. g. cloning animals like Dolly. Scientists in Asia are trying to clone humans, too. But the use of embryos and the consequences of such actions are questionable. Should humans interfere with life and play God?
- *Alternative:* Companies like Monsanto or AstraZeneca have created a new GM crop which they claim can help poor farmers in Africa and feed the world because it has better features. Many African countries criticise their business strategies. Their aim is to maximise profit. So is genetic engineering a blessing or a curse?

Pros (advantages):
- GM crops maximise yield as they have better characteristics (e. g. resistance to droughts). This is especially relevant in times of climate change, when some areas receive less rain.
- So they can be used to stop famine and to help poor countries feed their population. The population will reach 9 billion by 2050, GM crops can help to feed so many people.
- They help poor farmers because they do not risk losing all their harvest because of bad weather or pest. Farming becomes more predictable.
- GM products are well tested, they do not harm people. GM products can be healthier as they contain more nutrients.
- Genetic engineering offers new solutions, e. g. it can provide a cure for diseases such as Alzheimer's or Parkinson's disease.
- The embryos that are used are only days old, they do not count as human life. Often they are 'leftovers' from fertilisation efforts, which would be destroyed anyway.
- Both *Brave New World* and *Gattaca* show dystopian worlds. Both are fiction. The authors wrote them to point out the inherent dangers of genetic engineering. In *Gattaca*, we can see how an ordinary human transcends the limits of his society.

Cons (disadvantages/dangers):
- GM products (crops, cures) are expensive, companies only want to maximise profits.
- Expensive GM products are not available to poor people/countries. GM crops only make sense for huge agricultural corporations.
- If poor farmers buy GM products, they will have to take out a loan, which they cannot pay back if prices fall. So they could fall into debt and lose their farms.
- The consequences of GM crops are not well tested/unknown, there are potential dangers in the long run.
- GM crops pollute the environment, once GM food is grown, e. g. bees will pollinate GM seeds and 'ordinary' crops will be affected.
- Life is sacred/a gift of God and using embryos for genetic engineering is morally wrong. Man should not interfere with life.
- If GM is used on humans, as it is in this text or in the novel *Brave New World* and the film *Gattaca* the resulting humans are deprived of a free choice (*Brave New World*) or those who are not genetically modified do not have any chances of success in a highly regulated society (*Gattaca*).

Notizen

Conclusion: Sum up main fact(s) and give your opinion.
- **Fear:** Genetic engineering affects human life fundamentally. In my opinion it is immoral to use embryos for science and this should be forbidden. Besides the results of using GM crops are not well tested, nobody can predict the long-term consequences. Once GM crops are sown, other crops will be infested. So I do not approve of it at all.
- **Vision:** Genetic engineering is a powerful tool, which changes our lives. The consequences can be good or bad; we can manipulate the character traits of humans (like in this text or in *Brave New World* or in the film *Gattaca*) and deprive them of a choice. But it also promises cures for terrible diseases. It is a question of regulating GM research and trying to make sure it has no harmful effects. If one country bans genetic engineering, research will go on in another part of the world where rules are less strict. So we should determine which rules apply rather than condemning the whole technology area.

Notizen

Trainingsaufgabe 9

Aufgabentyp	Summary, comparison, discussion
Thema	Immigration to Canada, Canada as a Multicultural Society
Material	Margaret Davis: *New Beginnings*
Textsorte	Sachtext
Niveau	Grundkurs und Leistungskurs

Assignments

1. Summarise the text.

2. "Rather than expecting newcomers to abandon their own cultural heritage, the emphasis is on finding ways to integrate differences in a pluralistic society." Compare and contrast this attitude to the relationship between white Britons and immigrants from former colonies like the Caribbean or India. Refer to texts studied in class.

3. Compare the new type of immigration with immigration in the 19th century. Discuss the importance of immigrants for an information- and knowledge-based economy such as Canada's or Germany's and what should be done to integrate them successfully.

Material

Margaret Davis
New Beginnings

Jason Kenney sees immigrants as role models: "You observe how these new Canadians live their lives. They are the personification of Margaret Thatcher's aspirational class. They're all about a massive work ethic." [...] Yet Kenney also says that immigrants have a duty to integrate into Canadian society. In a 2010 speech to students at Huron University College in London, Ontario, the minister [for citizenship] noted that Canada, with a total population of 34 million people, accepts about 250,000 new permanent residents a year. [...] "How can a country that maintains such a high level of immigration, while embracing the diversity that it brings, maintain a sense of social cohesion, of common purpose and of national identity?", Kenney asked. [...] Still, the minister's calls for more integration are mild in comparison with recent debates in Germany and other parts of Europe. He is critical of immigrants forming parallel communities, but adds that these "are to some extent a natural, unavoidable and arguably even desirable part of the immigration experience as people come to an immigrant-receiving country and get settled by initially attaching themselves to communities with which they are familiar that provide social support [...]"

Founded by British and French settlers, Canada has been welcoming immigrants as a policy since the late 19th century. Initially, newcomers were encouraged to build the nation, clearing land for farms and working in forestry and mining. Today the country's needs are different: immigrants provide skilled labour for an information- and knowledge-based economy. [...] Canada will need more than 300,000 new immigrants a year after 2011, not including non-permanent workers and students.

How will these immigrants adjust to life in Canada? The 2001 Federal Immigrant Integration Strategy states that "newcomers are expected to understand and respect basic Canadian values, and Canadians are expected to understand and respect the cultural differences newcomers bring to Canada. Rather than expecting newcomers to abandon their own cultural heritage, the emphasis is on finding ways to integrate differences in a pluralistic society." An important road to the integration is learning one of Canada's two official languages. [...]

Since the early 1990s, Canada has seen an increase in temporary foreign workers entering the country. In 2006, for the first time, the number of such workers was greater than the number of permanent immigrants. While this means that employers can respond to labour shortages more quickly, the trend has its risks. [...] "[It] raises the possibility of creating a class of individuals who, as a result, are not full citizens and who run the risk of being 'ghettoized', as they have been in European countries, such as France [...]. What sets Canada´s temporary foreign-worker policies apart from policies in most of the rest of the world is that Canada permits long-term international workers to become permanent residents and, ultimately, citizens," notes the Conference Board. [...]

On 24 December 2009, four migrant workers were killed in Toronto when the scaffold they were standing on collapsed, and they fell more than 13 storeys to the ground. None of the men were wearing safety harnesses, according to the UFCW (United Food and Commercial Workers), a national union that speaks out for foreign workers in non-union positions. [...]

Diana MacKay, the Conference Board's director of education and health, agrees that temporary foreign workers are potentially at risk. "They are dependent on their employer and their new country to take good care of them, so if some of these safety nets fail to materialize when they need them, they´re vulnerable," MacKay says. "We need to do everything possible to ensure that exploitation doesn't occur, and where it does occur, to fix it rapidly and put in place additional mechanisms to ensure it doesn't happen again."

(617 words)

"New Beginnings" – © Business Spotlight 01/2011,
www.business-spotlight.de

Notizen

Lösungsvorschlag

Aufgabe 1

Summarise the text.

HINWEIS   Hier müssen Sie die Hauptaussagen des Textes prägnant zusammenfassen. Bitte zitieren Sie nicht wörtlich aus dem Text, sondern formulieren Sie einen eigenständigen Text. Verwenden Sie das *Simple Present*.

Lösungsschritte

1. Markieren Sie die wichtigen Aussagen des Textes.
2. Formulieren Sie einen einleitenden Satz (*umbrella sentence*), der Verfasserin, Quelle und Thema nennt.
3. Schreiben Sie nun Ihre Zusammenfassung – verzichten Sie auf Beispiele, Details oder Aufzählungen. Lösen Sie sich vom Originaltext.
4. Achten Sie darauf, logische Zusammenhänge deutlich zu machen, indem Sie z. B. Konjunktionen benutzen.
5. Verbessern Sie beim erneuten Lesen Fehler.

Stichpunktlösung

- Umbrella sentence: The report "New Beginnings" by Margaret Davis, published in the magazine *Spotlight* 1 / 2011, describes the attitudes of Canadians concerning immigrants and integration,
- Canada accepts a great number of new permanent residents each year.
- Jason Kenney (Minister of Citizenship) is critical of parallel societies and calls for more integration, while at the same time acknowledging the sense of security, which immigrants might draw from living among other people with the same language – he praises the immigrants' will to work hard,
- unlike the farmers and miners needed to settle in the country in the 19th century, Canada needs skilled immigrants in the 21st century to cater for the labour needs of its knowledge-based industries,
- integration in Canada works two ways, immigrants are expected to respect Canadian values and speak one of its official languages, while the Canadian society must respect their cultural differences,
- apart from permanent residents, Canada also accepts temporary foreign workers, who are at risk of being excluded socially; there have been reports of poor safety at work and trade unions are concerned about protecting them from being exploited,
- nevertheless, Canada offers even long-term foreign workers the possibility of becoming permanent residents.

LÖSUNG: TRAININGSAUFGABE 9

Aufgabe 2

"Rather than expecting newcomers to abandon their own cultural heritage, the emphasis is on finding ways to integrate differences in a pluralistic society." **Compare and contrast** this attitude to the relationship between white Britons and immigrants from former colonies like the Caribbean or India. Refer to texts studied in class.

HINWEIS   In dieser Aufgabe sollten Sie zunächst kurz die Haltung, die dem Zitat zugrunde liegt, erläutern. Stellen Sie die genannten Punkte dann einem oder mehreren Texten aus dem Unterricht gegenüber.

Lösungsschritte

1. Stellen Sie die im Text genannte Haltung klar dar.
2. Beziehen Sie sich auf die Texte, die Sie im Unterricht behandelt haben. Bei der Auswahl der Texte sind Sie völlig frei. (Auch Filme wie etwa *East is East* oder *My Beautiful Laundrette* könnten herangezogen werden.) Stellen Sie Ihre Gemeinsamkeiten oder Unterschiede möglichst präzise dar und führen Sie Beispiele an (wichtige Charaktere/aussagekräftige Situationen).
3. Stellen Sie am Ende nochmals beide Konstellationen (Immigranten im Vereinigten Königreich – Immigranten in Kanada) gegenüber und ziehen Sie eine Schlussfolgerung, die sich aus Ihrem Text ergibt.
4. Verbessern Sie beim erneuten Lesen Fehler.

Stichpunktlösung

Comparison Canada – Great Britain
- Canada: newcomers are not expected to give up their own culture,
- their contribution is seen as enriching,
- even parallel societies, while not entirely welcome, are tolerated as a step on the way to integration,
- requirement for immigrants: language skills in one official language (English or French),
- Canada encourages immigration. (250,000 new immigrants per year),
- numbers will rise to fill labour shortages,
- country is not densely populated (34 million inhabitants),
- country needs and can accommodate skilled immigrants (qualifications determine who can immigrate),
- even temporary workers get a chance to become citizens after a set period of time,
- immigrants are seen as an 'aspirational class' (work hard in order to reach social mobility),
- if immigrants recognize their chance of success, they are willing to integrate and work hard,
- immigrants from all countries are welcome, whether or not they have ties with the Anglo-French community,
- Great Britain: citizens of former colonies were officially permitted to settle in Britain after World War II,
- many of them spoke some English (with a regional accent),

Notizen

- immigrants from Caribbean islands considered themselves 'British' and were surprised by the hostility of white Britons (opposed to Canadian openness).

Hostility towards Caribbean immigrants: Andrea Levy's novel *Small Island*
- British culture and language = considered superior to own culture in colonies,
- immigrants hope to have a better life and become members of a more privileged class (for example Hortense),
- she is treated as a second class citizen and her qualification as a teacher is not valued,
- taxi driver does not understand her accent. Neither does she understand his working class London dialect,
- she is surprised by the dismal post-war living conditions in London.

Immigration from India, Pakistan:
Exotic success and everyday racism: Hanif Kureishi's novel *The Buddha of Suburbia*
- Haroon (narrator Karim's father) comes to the UK in 1950 to complete his education,
- he comes from a wealthy Indian family,
- he fails to graduate from university and starts work as an office clerk,
- Karim describes his father as charming and more attractive than most English people,
- he becomes the exotic attraction of his London suburb when he starts his new career as a spiritual yoga instructor,
- Karim's father is a successful immigrant, who faces few problems,
- meanwhile his friends, Uncle Anwar and Auntie Jeeta ("an Indian princess") are faced with everyday racism as owners of a corner shop,
- their daughter Jamila becomes a radical fighter for equal rights,
- she accuses Karim of lacking awareness of his cultural roots,
- despite their middle or upper-class roots in India or Pakistan, many immigrants are perceived as poor and uncultured by English (Karim's ironic comment: "it was said they were not familiar with cutlery and certainly not with toilets, since they squatted on the seats and shat from on high", Hanif Kureishi: *The Buddha of Suburbia*, London: Faber and Faber, 1990, p. 24),
- many are forced to work in low-qualified jobs such as owners of corner shops, conductors on buses or as taxi drivers.

Young immigrants embracing their Muslim roots: Hanif Kureishi's short story *My Son the Fanatic*
- The father (taxi driver) enjoys the British lifestyle and does everything for his son to succeed in British society,
- his son becomes a radical Muslim and gives up his Western lifestyle,
- he accuses his father of compromising his culture and embracing a hostile Western culture unthinkingly,
- this conflict about how far integration should go remains unresolved, the story ends with a question.

Notizen

Hard work and ambitious parents: *Bend it like Beckham*
- Second and third generation: ambitious parents try to make their children work hard for a successfully integrated future as doctors or lawyers (example of 'aspirational class' quoted in the text),
- yet, their traditions should be respected (cooking, clothes, arranged marriages),
- Jesminder's professional dream: play soccer and go to US to play soccer at university,
- her personal dream: love relationship with her Irish coach,
- parents comply eventually (conflict is resolved in favour of integration).

Conclusion
- British society today is truly multicultural (Robin Cook's "Chicken Tikka Masala speech"; chicken tikka masala = an Indian dish with a new kind of sauce to accommodate English tastes), but there are various degrees of assimilation,
- the measure of integration in Britain differs sharply between different ethnic groups (e. g. Pakistani immigrants are less likely to succeed economically than other groups),
- Canada successfully integrates immigrants by allowing cultural differences as long as they accept basic values and communicate in English/French.

THE DYNAMICS OF CHANGE

Aufgabe 3

Compare the new type of immigration with immigration in the 19th century. **Discuss** the importance of immigrants for an information- and knowledge-based economy such as Canada's or Germany's and what should be done to integrate them successfully.

HINWEIS Achten Sie auf die Zweiteilung der Aufgabe. Stellen Sie zunächst die Entwicklung dar und erläutern Sie dann die Rolle der Migranten in der Informationsgesellschaft. Sie sollen am Schluss Stellung beziehen, vermeiden Sie aber polarisierende Aussagen zu diesem sensiblen Thema.

Lösungsschritte

1. Sie könnten in der Einleitung auf kontroverse Beiträge zur Integrationsdebatte verweisen oder sachlich einsteigen (z. B. Statistiken aus dem Text zitieren).
2. Stellen Sie kurz die Entwicklung in Kanada vom 19. zum 21. Jahrhundert dar (von „Kolonisation" zu Wissensökonomie).
3. Im Anschluss sollten Sie die Gemeinsamkeiten zwischen Kanada und Deutschland als hoch entwickelte Länder darstellen und die Rolle von Migranten in einer Wissensgesellschaft diskutieren.
4. Erörtern Sie, welche Voraussetzungen gegeben sein müssen, damit Integration von Migranten erfolgreich sein kann. (Hierbei kann der Text Ihnen einige Anhaltspunkte geben.)
5. Verbessern Sie beim erneuten Lesen Fehler.

Stichpunktlösung

Importance of immigrants in Canada and Germany
Introduction:
- Debate in Germany: Angela Merkel's speech on failed integration (lacking language skills, parallel societies),
- Thilo Sarrazin's controversial theses (racist assumption of inferior intelligence),
- Canada: traditionally welcoming to immigrants, relies on their contribution,
- 250,000 new immigrants each year; numbers expected to rise.

From 19th to 21st century:
- 19th century Canada: Immigrants were needed to work in mining and clear land and settle new farms ("roughing it in the bush"),
- primary industries,
- rough adventurous type, prepared to live in simple living conditions and faced with a harsh cold climate,
- result: development of infrastructure and economy in Canada,
- new settlers often experience personal frustration and resignation,
- keyword: "survival" (Margaret Atwood) as first and only goal,
- opposed to 'frontier' ("utopia", "conquering new land", "unlimited possibilities") or "American Dream" ("life, liberty and the pursuit of happiness").

21st century = knowledge-based society:
- Canada is a highly developed, wealthy country,
- GDP (PPP) per person roughly $ 40 000, slightly higher than in Germany (roughly 36,000 per capita),
- HDI 0,888 = very high human development index (measures education, health) = similar to Germany,
- Canada and Germany: rely on globalised world for imports of goods,
- Canada: rich in raw materials (unlike Germany),
- skilled immigrants are needed for service sector as well as knowledge sector (in both countries),
- language knowledge and professional skills are vital in order to succeed in these jobs,
- Germany: demographic trend will lead to a lack of young people, imbalance in population (too many old people),
- this endangers the welfare state (too many (elderly) people rely on help),
- knowledge driven economy needs experts in engineering, IT and the care sector,
- the lack of qualified workers endangers economic growth and ability to compete on the world market,
- immigration could help to solve Germany´s demographic problem.
- How to attract the kind of immigrants needed in an information-based economy?
- The country must offer them attractive working conditions and a possibility to succeed,
- there should be institutions to help them develop their basic language skills,
- one must create a tolerant atmosphere where well-educated immigrants feel welcome,
- this was not done in the 60s and 70s, when low-skilled workers were invited to fill the gap in the German workforce,
- as a consequence, they have not always integrated into German society – in some cases (especially with women) their language skills are poor,
- a new kind of policy (possibly similar to Canada's) is necessary.

Trainingsaufgabe 10

Aufgabentyp	Summary, interpretation, discussion
Thema	Science and technology: Models of the Future
Material	*New technology too advanced for own good.* In: *Daily Collegian, University of Massachusetts internet student newspaper*
Textsorte	Sachtext
Niveau	Grundkurs

Assignments

1. Summarise the text.

2. Illustrate the problems and implications of the VeriChip by referring to your reading (and viewing) experience concerning models of the future.

3. Discuss the importance of personal freedom and its limits taking into account the importance of freedom in the American Dream.

Material

New technology too advanced for own good (October 18, 2004)
An editorial from the Massachusetts internet student newspaper *Daily Collegian*. Unsigned editorials represent the majority opinion of the *Daily Collegian* Editorial Board.

The Food and Drug Administration recently approved Applied Digital Solutions, a technology company based in Florida, to market microchips intended for implantation under the skin in humans to allow easier access for a person's medical records. This concept has been met with much hesitation, especially when seen from the point of view that Orwell had brought up with his novel 1984 which depicted Big Brother watching over everyone at all times. This technology, however, can be most helpful in saving a person's life when it comes to paramedics and EMTs making split-second decisions. With all the potential and theoretical good it could bring to the world of emergency medicine, the scary proceedings that could result from this kind of technology are far too dangerous for society to explore.
Going by the theory that Applied Digital has, the benefits in emergency medicine that this product has to offer are too great to ignore. According to the New York Times, the chip would be implanted under the skin of a person's arm or hand via syringe and would not contain any detailed medical records, but rather, a number which would be linked to a medical directory. The medical records, which would contain information about the patient concerning their blood type, drug histories, and major surgeries/diseases the patient has had or currently has, would be updated quite frequently and very easily. The device used by emergency medical personnel to read the exclusive 16-digit number on each chip would be a hand[-]held radio scanner.

This technology could be very useful when used with the intention that it was approved for. If a person passes out while jogging one day, EMTs and paramedics would still be able to find out the person's drug allergies, past medical history, and current medications even with the patient unconscious. Thus, all the appropriate medical treatments could be administered without worrying about the patient having an allergic reaction to a drug and, even possibly, determining what caused the patient to pass out based on their past medical history (ex: if the patient is hypoglycemic and their glucose level dropped too low which accounted for them going unconscious). The VeriChip, as the implanted microchip is commonly called, could greatly decrease the amount of malpractice encountered in the field. However, with all the good and promise the VeriChip holds for emergency medicine, the thought and future prospects of where the implanted chip will lead society in years to come is too frightening when it comes to maintaining people's privacies. One major concern brought up by the prospect of the VeriChip is that this technology is currently being used as a security feature. Rafael Macedo de la Concha, the attorney general of Mexico, has received, in addition to many of his subordinates, an implanted chip controlling security access to a secure room containing highly-confidential documents vital in Mexico's battle with the drug cartels. If this technology continues to expand with its methods of use, we will soon be checking out library books by scanning our wrists instead of our library cards.

While the intentions are certainly noble with regards to the emergency medical profession, the logistics of the VeriChip are taking us into worlds that have only been seen in novels such as 1984 and Aldous Huxley's Brave New World and in movies such as Gattica [sic!] and Minority Report. The fear of the chip being implanted in people is centered on the idea of authorities using it to keep track of its citizens. And while this may not necessarily be the case yet, the foot is in the door and this scenario is inevitable if this technology is further developed and made readily available through implantations in humans.

(615 words)

http://www.infowars.com/print/science/newtech.htm [zuletzt aufgerufen am 31.05.2012]

Lösungsvorschlag

Aufgabe 1

Summarise the text.

Lösungsschritte

1. Unterstreichen Sie die Kernaussagen im Text.
2. Formulieren Sie einen einleitenden Satz (*umbrella sentence*), in dem Sie Autor, Titel, Quelle und Thema nennen.
3. Fassen Sie nun die Kernaussagen in eigenen Worten zusammen, achten Sie auf die Verwendung des Simple Present.
4. Lesen Sie Ihre Zusammenfassung nochmals genau durch und korrigieren Sie Fehler. (Achten Sie dabei auf Zeitformen.)

Stichpunktlösung

- Author of the editorial "New technology too advanced for own good" is concerned with the rapid advance of technology in the field of digital technology/data storage,
- example in the text is the so-called VeriChip,
- chip can be implanted under a patient's skin and is readable using a scanner, contains a 16-digit number providing a link to a database which holds information about a patient's medical data (blood type, drug history, past operations),
- information like this can ensure proper treatment of a patient in case of accident,
- text also highlights the problematical aspects of such a technological development, as VeriChip technology is not restricted to medical issues,
- author asks if this technology – once established in specific fields such as medical treatment and security – might be expanded to other fields,
- implants containing personal data and the corresponding technology to read this information can swiftly lead to a threat to personal privacy,
- examples given in the text refer to fictional texts, in particular to the films *Minority Report* and *Gattica* [sic!] as well as Orwell's seminal dystopian novel *1984*.

Aufgabe 2

Illustrate the problems and implications of the VeriChip by referring to your reading (and viewing) experience concerning models of the future.

Lösungsschritte

1. Fertigen Sie eine Stoffsammlung zu möglichen Problemen und Konsequenzen der VeriChip-Technologie an. Gehen Sie vom Text aus und nennen Sie weitere Punkte. Finden Sie Belege aus Texten, die Sie im Unterricht gelesen haben (im letzten Absatz werden verschiedene mögliche Referenzen genannt).
2. Leiten Sie zum Thema hin, indem Sie kurz auf gesellschaftliche Tendenzen hinweisen, die zum VeriChip führen.

3. Denken Sie daran, möglichst detaillierte Parallelen zwischen den im Text angedeuteten Problemen und dem Unterrichtsmaterial herzustellen.
4. Achten Sie beim erneuten Lesen auf Fehler.

Stichpunktlösung

The following general implications and problems could be discussed in the analysis.

Individual freedom
- Widespread use of VeriChip technology implies that people have to give up specific civil rights, e.g. the right to withhold personal data from authorities,
- VeriChip technology enables authorities to access virtually any kind of personal data without a person's consent if it is stored on an implant,
- the consequence could be widespread data mining. Data can be gathered, compared and processed, which could lead to possible abuse and manipulation.

Examples from fictional texts
- Fictional and non-fictional texts that can be discussed in this context should be adequately referred to,
- in the film *Gattaca*, for example, personal information determines the future life of each citizen. In this example the most private information – DNA – can be read out and is used for both security and social planning,
- a critical view of the process of technological perfection is portrayed in Aldous Huxley's novel *Brave New World*; family, cultural diversity, art, literature, science, religion and philosophy have been abolished for the sake of technological perfection.

Wider reaching implications regarding law enforcement
- "3-strikes legislation" in the U.S.: This procedure (which enables authorities to sentence convicts ever more severely after three successive felonies) has been criticised, as there were cases in which a convict was sent to jail for 25 years after stealing chocolate chip cookies. He had previously committed armed burglary and assault, which together would not have earned such a sentence. VeriChip technology could enable such a process to be accomplished even more swiftly, thus complicating the already controversial debate about this kind of legislation.

Aufgabe 3

Discuss the importance of personal freedom and its limits taking into account the importance of freedom in the American Dream.

Lösungsschritte

1. Machen Sie sich Notizen zum Thema Freiheit im Allgemeinen und zu ihrer Bedeutung in der amerikanischen Gesellschaft (z. B. *Declaration of Independence*). Welche Arten der Freiheit kennen wir (religiöse oder politische Freiheit, Meinungsfreiheit usw.)?
2. Erläutern Sie die Definition von Freiheit im jeweiligen Kontext. Nehmen Sie auch auf den vorliegenden Text Bezug (Überwachungsstaat).

Notizen

ORDER, VISION AND CHANGE

3. Verfassen Sie nun Ihre Erörterung mit Einleitung, Hauptteil und Schluss. Achten Sie darauf, Ihre Gedanken zu verbinden.
4. In der Schlussfolgerung müssen Sie zu einer begründeten Stellungnahme gelangen, die auf den vorhergehenden Überlegungen beruht.
5. Lesen Sie den Text erneut und verbessern Sie eventuell Fehler. Denken Sie hierbei besonders an Zeiten und Wortstellung.

Stichpunktlösung

Introduction
- Freedom is a basic human right,
- people in Western societies value personal freedom highly, e. g. the freedom to choose a job you like, to live with the person you love, to express your opinion, to travel,
- this concept is deeply engrained in American society,
- the first settlers were searching for religious freedom.

Religious freedom
- Originally the "American Dream" was a religious dream,
- search for the "New Jerusalem" where Puritans could practise their religion freely,
- Puritan societies exerted a rigid form of social control over their members to conform to Puritan rules,
- people who broke these rules were excluded from the community (e. g. Nathaniel Hawthorne's *The Scarlet Letter* or Arthur Miller's *The Crucible*, based on the *Salem Witch Hunt*),
- both books condemn religious narrow-mindedness and bigotry,
- the Puritans' understanding of freedom meant religious freedom but not personal freedom, if personal choices were incompatible with Puritan beliefs (e. g. love outside marriage),
- personal freedom to choose your belief and to follow your conscience should be as important as religious freedom.

Life, liberty and the pursuit of happiness (Declaration of Independence)
- The first document states the new country's values: life, liberty and the pursuit of happiness,
- freedom means personal freedom and the pursuit of happiness means the possibility to pursue your own happiness, e. g. to define what makes you happy and to reach this goal,
- the freedom to dissent is deeply engrained in the American psyche (Henry David Thoreau refused to pay taxes for an unjust war and was sent to prison, but he was also one of the most influential thinkers of the 19th century),
- heroes of American films and fiction are often outcasts, who do not follow social conventions (*Dances with Wolves*, *Forrest Gump*, Bruce Willis in *Die Hard*).

Trapped in the dangers of the genetic manipulation: *Brave New World*
- The World State opposes the values of American society,
- values of the World State: "identity, community, stability",
- identity means lower castes consists of identical twins (Bokanovsky groups),

Notizen

- sleep teaching ensures that people are happy with their place in the social hierarchy,
- there is no individuality, people are part of a community,
- there is no ambition or upward mobility and no quest for freedom or individuality because they would make society less stable,
- society is more important than individual and personal freedom.

Overcoming the dangers of genetic surveillance: *Gattaca*
- Genetically enhanced babies are the rule and naturally born children are disadvantaged,
- screening for risks happens at birth and determines a person's life chances,
- protagonist cannot realise his ambition to become an astronaut because of genetic limitations,
- he has to work as a cleaner,
- when he assumes a new identity of a 'perfectly' manipulated individual, he meets all requirements and realises his dream,
- the individual transcends social and genetic limits,
- a perfect example of the "American Dream".

Conclusion: Material happiness and the limits of growth
- For many people today the "American Dream" means material well-being, a house in the suburbs, a car, and the freedom to consume,
- this dream is socially and ecologically unsustainable,
- the financial crisis has shown that American affluence was based on borrowed money,
- believing that house prices would continue to rise, people borrowed money to finance a lifestyle they could not really afford,
- now Americans are faced with huge debts, lots of homes have been repossessed and people have had to wake up from their dream,
- the future of America looks less optimistic with new economies such as India and China taking jobs in manufacturing, creating a new middle-class imitating Western lifestyles and striving for dominance in the 21st century,
- the 'American way of life' causes too many greenhouse gases and uses up too many of our natural resources,
- it causes climate change, a depletion of natural resources, the extinction of species and disasters such as the Deepwater Horizon accident (dependence on oil),
- this endangers human survival,
- there must be limits to personal freedom, people must lead sustainable lives to ensure human survival.

IDEALS AND REALITY

Trainingsaufgabe 11

Aufgabentyp	Summary, characterisation, comparison, discussion
Thema	Emotional influence of the media: TV violence in daily life
Material	Joyce Carol Oates: *Love, Forever*. In: W. Martin (ed.): *More Stories We Tell. The Best Contemporary Short Stories by North American Women*.
Textsorte	Kurzgeschichte
Niveau	Leistungskurs

Assignments

1. Summarize the text.
2. Characterize the protagonist and analyse the implications of the title in reference to the text.
3. Compare the heroine in Oates'[s] story to a Shakespearean protagonist of your choice and decide whether Oates'[s] main character is a "tragic heroine".
4. The right to possess guns (as guaranteed by the US Constitution) has been a matter of recent discussion. Explore the pros and cons of this issue and express your opinion.

Material

Joyce Carol Oates
Love, Forever

He was crazy about her and certainly behaved that way when they were together, and alone. But he wasn't crazy about her three kids. It isn't anything personal, he said, but I'm not the type, y'know?
She was gazing hurt, eyes brimming with tears deep into his eyes. But said, softly, I
5 know.
Framing his face in her hands like an actress gazing into those blue eyes like sapphires whispering another time, I know, and solemnly she'd kissed his lips and he'd remember it, that kiss: that kiss he could not guess was a pledge.
Oh, I know! – but I love you anyway forever.
10 The entire day, the sun was hidden behind clouds, one of those gauzy days you feel like screaming but she was calm, she was in control. She's been smiling all day. It wasn't practice, it was her natural self: as, in high school, she'd smiled all the time. She was waiting for a phone call and when it came she had something planned to say she'd memorized, a strange man prowling the woods behind the trailer, she wasn't worried

really, but she'd mention it, then talk of something else. Not too much detail - that gave you away. From TV you learned that.

She called him, too: knowing he wouldn't be home. Just to hear his voice on the answering tape - that was enough.

No message.

She had the gun ready. A guy had given her it for protection, when she'd moved out here alone with the kids. She knew where to toss it where nobody would find it. She put on old rubber gloves she'd be throwing away, too. She was wearing a warm sweatshirt. It was eleven p.m. and the kids were sleeping, a dark night with no moon and everything quiet back in the woods. She hadn't even had the TV on. Tommy, who was so excitable, naturally had to be first. She went into his room, holding the pistol calmly, she whispered, Sweetie? as she'd planned to wake him so he'd be looking up, and when he opened his eyes she pulled the trigger. Jesus, what a noise! - Her ears ringing. Tommy died at once, she believed. A bullet point-blank through his chest, thus no suffering. She'd planned that.

Next was Sherri, four years old. Pale blond hair and her mommy's button nose. Sherri slept in Mommy's bedroom where the baby was also, and the noise had been so loud Sherri was out of bed, screaming. Mommy? Mommy? - and she ran inside, trying to stay calm, swallowing, but her voice rising shrill, It's okay, honey! Mommy's here! And she fired at the little girl, it wasn't exactly clear what happened but there was one bullet in the chest yet more screaming, and a second bullet in the chest and still more screaming, and now she was maybe losing it just a little, panting, stooping over the fallen writhing child to press the barrel against the top of the child's head and to squeeze the trigger again.

And the baby. In his crib, in the corner of the room - that wasn't going to be hard! He had wakened of course but hadn't begun yet to cry. It was that kind of baby - a little slow.

At the hospital she ran inside screaming. A man, a man shot my kids! And they came out at once, no wasting time, and saw Tommy in the front seat, and pulled him out to try to save his life, My God there's a baby - one of the orderlies yelled, like he couldn't believe it, and she stood there watching, this little smile on her face, bemused - how they were all running around, not smooth and coordinated the way you'd expect, taking the kids inside to save their lives when, couldn't they tell? - these kids were dead. Actually, in fact, Tommy was not dead, but dying: he'd die, officially at four a.m. of the next day.

The baby was dead.

It had been a listless baby, conceived not in love but spite.

So much commotion in the emergency unit, everybody gaping, like lights had come on brighter like on TV, and maybe in fact they had, and she was standing there, watching, in her blood-soaked clothes, her new jeans tight, and her Led Zeppelin sweatshirt, and the spike-heeled glamour boots - she was blinking, smiling just faintly, as if all she was doing was watching, calm, and curious to see how it would go, as the medical crew would testify at her trial. Where she should have been - what? Screaming, sobbing? - was that what another mother would do, in this situation? Or was she, you could argue this, in shock?

But, no, she was reported to have called out, Nothing but the best for these kids! And she'd sounded scolding, but sly. Her eyes making the rounds of the waiting room where everybody's eyes were sure on her.

But then, my God, it came to her like a blow: little Sherri was still in the car!

Nobody'd seen Sherri. She must have slipped off the backseat during the wild ride to town, and the goddamn careless medical crew hadn't even noticed. So, she was excited now, she had to yell to get their attention, Hey, my little girl! – don't forget her.
The look on their faces. Almost, you'd have to laugh.
It was weird, though, and she'd never understand it – forgetting Sherri like that. Sherri was the one Mommy had always loved best.

(855 words)

Oates, Joyce Carol, Love, Forever, from: More Stories We Tell. The Best Contemporary Short Stories by North American Women, edited by Wendy Martin, Knopf Publishing Group, New York, 2004, pages 142-145

LÖSUNG: TRAININGSAUFGABE 11

Lösungsvorschlag

Aufgabe 1

Summarize the text.

HINWEIS   Die formalen Bedingungen einer Inhaltswiedergabe müssen beachtet werden: *present tense*; keine Zitate/direkte Rede/Kommentar; sprachliches Anpassen der Verweise auf Ort, Zeit und Personen; Textlänge ist ca. ¼ bis ⅓ des Originals; *umbrella sentence* (Angabe von Ort, Zeit, Autor, Titel, Thema).

Lösungsschritte

1. Markieren Sie die Kernaussagen im Text.
2. Beginnen Sie die Zusammenfassung mit einem einleitenden Satz (*umbrella sentence*). Nennen Sie Autorin, Titel und Thema.
3. Fassen Sie nun die Handlung in eigenen Worten zusammen, ohne Details zu nennen. Verwenden Sie das *Simple Present*.
4. Lesen Sie den Text erneut kritisch durch und verbessern Sie mögliche Fehler.

Stichpunktlösung

Story deals with the determining force of TV violence:
- young woman living in trailer park – told by lover that he loves her but not her children – pledges love in return – plans murder of children with handgun,
- kills all three children, son, daughter and baby – daughter Sherri most difficult because awake,
- takes bodies to hospital – claims stranger from woods has killed them – watches emergency crew fighting for Tommy's life – suddenly remembers Sherri is in car – blames medical crew for being careless,
- Sherri was most-loved child.

Aufgabe 2

Characterize the protagonist and **analyse** the implications of the title in reference to the text.

Lösungsschritte

1. Lesen Sie den Text erneut, um aus dem Verhalten der Protagonistin Rückschlüsse auf ihren Charakter zu ziehen. Markieren Sie relevante Passagen, um sie später anzuführen.
2. Verfassen Sie eine Charakterisierung, belegen Sie Ihre Behauptungen durch Bezüge zum Text.
3. Analysieren Sie nun den Titel und beziehen Sie die Begriffe *love* und *forever* auf den Text. Um welche Arten von Liebe geht es, welcher Konflikt entsteht aus der Liebe zu einem Mann und der Liebe zu den Kindern? Was bedeutet *forever*?
4. Korrigieren Sie beim zweiten Lesen Fehler.

Stichpunktlösung

Protagonist:
- young American woman – high school educated – recently divorced or separated – lives with three children in trailer park near woods,
- superficial – always smiling – behaves like person imitating character from TV series – e.g. holds his face in her hands "like an actress" (l. 6),
- looks after herself – wears new jeans, Led Zeppelin sweatshirt, glamour boots,
- started new relationship – lover does not want her children – she decides to murder them – knows how from TV/films – has gun – plans alibi – premeditated murder,
- murders planned and executed in highly dramatic way – alibi phone calls copied from TV (l. 16) – calls lover's answering machine "Just to hear his voice on the answering tape" (ll. 17/18).

Title:
- "Love, Forever" – romantic pledge – "I love you anyway forever" (l. 9) – and beginning of plan to kill children,
- different meanings of "love" and "forever" and role they play in the text – love for lover vs. love for children,
- conflict between lovers would normally lead to breakdown of relationship – love could "anyway" continue forever – kiss could then be seen as parting pledge,
- protagonist takes different interpretation – "forever" means eternally, longer than life – taken literally – conflict between love and life – love as superior value to life – pledge as dream of happy end after children's death – overly romantic view – TV etc. – sees herself as justified in killing children,
- maternal love – children as evidence of love – also to protagonist – Tommy/Sherri/baby as different evidence – protagonist loves baby least – baby "conceived not in love but spite" (l. 51),
- loves Sherri best – same sex – similar features – "mommy's button nose" (l. 30) – trembles, her voice rising shrill, "she was maybe losing it" (l. 36), when she kills Sherri.

Final sentence:
- – "Sherri was the one Mommy had always loved best" (ll. 68/69) – rounds off story in macabre sense – shows protagonist capable of love.

Aufgabe 3

Compare the heroine in Oates'[s] story to a Shakespearean protagonist of your choice and decide whether Oates'[s] main character is a "tragic heroine".

Lösungsschritte

1. Notieren Sie Gemeinsamkeiten und Unterschiede zwischen der Mutter und einem Shakespeare-Helden (Macbeth oder Hamlet bieten sich an, auch Lady Macbeth wäre denkbar).
2. Gehen Sie in Ihrer Einleitung auf Begriffe wie Tragödie bzw. tragischer Held ein.

3. Formulieren Sie nun einen klar strukturierten Text, der die Protagonistin mit einem Shakespeare-Charakter vergleicht. Achten Sie darauf, nicht nur gelerntes Shakespeare-Wissen abzuspulen. Je genauer Sie dabei auf weitere Begriffe der Dramenanalyse (z. B. Hybris, Fallhöhe) eingehen, desto besser.
4. Lesen Sie den Text nochmals durch und verbessern Sie ihn.

Stichpunktlösung

Shakespearean protagonists:
- many fit definition of tragic hero – all suffer from clash of reason and emotion,
- Hamlet – ambitious young nobleman – inability to resolve conflict situations leads him to tragic end – noble aim of revenge for father's death – unable to rationalise situation appropriately – kills Polonius by accident – becomes victim of tragic dilemma he has steered himself into because of his character weakness,
- Macbeth – noble person – driven by promise of supernatural powers – wife's ambition that he should become king – follows witches' promise literally – has present king killed to achieve his aim – feels vulnerable as King of Scotland – compelled to get rid of anyone who may suspect him or threaten his crown – when showdown comes, he sees no other solution than his own death – life ends tragically.

Oates's protagonist:
- failed personality – no tragic dilemma like Hamlet – her problem affects many relationships – vital but common choice – she takes easy way out by callously killing children – other available solutions would be more plausible/appropriate – her solution means end of her children, not her own tragic end – she expects happy end,
- similarity with Shakespeare – tragic personality weakness in protagonist – imbalance of reason/emotion leads to her living in unreal world – mental/emotional confusion of values – total conditioning by romantic images,
- actions of Oates' protagonist do not fulfil definition of tragic heroine – but from psychological point of view the tragic weakness within her personality might be seen as doing so.

Aufgabe 4

The right to possess guns (as guaranteed by the US Constitution) has been a matter of recent discussion. **Explore the pros and cons** of this issue and **express your opinion**.

Lösungsschritte

1. Strukturieren Sie Ihr Wissen zum Thema Waffen/Waffenbesitz. Denken Sie auch an historische Fakten, wie z. B. die Besiedlung des Westens.
2. Formulieren Sie eine Einleitung zum Thema mit möglichst aktuellem Bezug (z. B. *school shootings*, politische Attentate).
3. Stellen Sie Pro und Kontra dar, belegen Sie Ihre Thesen möglichst durch Beispiele oder Statistiken (z. B. zur Kriminalitätsrate). Verbinden Sie Ihre Gedanken durch Konnektoren (*on the one hand ... on the other hand*, *while*, *however*, *although*).

Notizen

IDEALS AND REALITY

4. Im Schlussteil müssen Sie zu einer begründeten Meinungsäußerung gelangen. Beziehen Sie sich dabei auf die von Ihnen dargestellten Fakten.
5. Achten Sie beim erneuten Lesen auf Fehlerkorrektur.

Stichpunktlösung

HINWEIS Die Lösung dieser Aufgabe erlaubt verschiedene Strategien. Vergessen Sie jedoch nicht, Ihre Argumente durch geeignete Beispiele aus der amerikanischen Geschichte und der gegenwärtigen Situation der USA zu stützen.

Recent discussion:
- right to bear arms – private ownership of guns – guaranteed by American constitution – highly controversial – massacres in US schools and elsewhere – high murder rate (currently over 16,000 per year nationwide).

Arguments for gun ownership:
- long history: right guaranteed in constitution (Bill of Rights, 1789 – pioneers/settlers had to provide own defence in undeveloped country – often beyond the law – hence "basic civil right" seen as basic aspect of American definition of "freedom"),
- young country unable to finance professional army – reliance on "privately armed local militias" – War of Independence against Britain, war against Mexico over Texas – Civil War = defending independence, defence of new country, saving the union,
- today, self-defence in cities – high percentage of violent crime,
- political influence of National Rifle Association (NRA) – major source of finance,
- terrorist attacks (bombing in Oklahoma – "9/11") – increased feeling of insecurity and need for self-defence.

Arguments against gun ownership:
- huge number of guns in private ownership – average of three per family – massacres in schools, neighbourhoods, firms, families facilitated partly by ease of buying and possessing guns – gun ownership seen as "natural" and "manly" (see Michael Moore's film *Bowling for Columbine*),
- accidental killing of innocents – children find guns at home – use them as toys,
- killing seen as natural part of life (= devaluation of concept of "value of life") – decline in ethical standards and values – basic human right of life as guaranteed in Declaration of Independence perverted,
- murder regarded as a means of solving one's problems, see text,
- rising violent crime rate in USA – economic and social problems such as unemployment, high immigration, outsourcing of jobs etc. demand new strategies – must go beyond just talk and banning guns (red herring).

Conclusion:
- should include one's own position on the right to possess guns – refer to specific examples.

Notizen

Trainingsaufgabe 12

Aufgabentyp	Mediation
Thema	Immigration in the United Kingdom
Material	Armin Laschet: *Von den Zuwanderern lernen*. In: *Die Zeit*
Textsorte	Zeitungsartikel
Niveau	Leistungskurs

Assignments

The article below was written by the Minister for Integration of North Rhine-Westphalia, Armin Laschet.
As a personal aide to the minister, it is your task to prepare a statement in English which summarises his key arguments for a panel discussion at the German Embassy in London. The participants in this discussion have been provided with four questions in advance. These questions are designed as guidelines for their statement and they are given here in German.

- Kann man westliche Gesellschaften als „multikulturell" bezeichnen?
- Braucht eine multikulturelle Gesellschaft eine Art „Leitkultur"? Oder sollte sie andersartige Werte und Lebensstile uneingeschränkt als gleichwertig tolerieren?
- Worin bestehen Wertvorstellungen und Normen, die für Ihr Verständnis von gesellschaftlichem Zusammenleben unverzichtbar sind?
- Welche Herausforderungen stellt die Entwicklung einer „Leitkultur" für die einheimische Bevölkerung dar?

Prepare the Minister's statement **in English** that reflects what he wrote in his article. The statement should focus on the four questions which have to be answered by him during the panel discussion in London.

Material

Armin Laschet
Von den Zuwanderern lernen

Sind wir für oder gegen eine multikulturelle Gesellschaft? Diese Frage bewegt seit langem die Gemüter in Deutschland. Doch warum eigentlich? Bei genauerer Betrachtung entpuppt sich der Erkenntniswert dieser Frage als äußerst mager – ähnlich wie bei der Überlegung, ob wir für oder gegen die Globalisierung sind. Wer mit offenen Augen
5 durchs Leben geht, sieht tagtäglich, dass viele Kulturen seit Jahrzehnten bei uns leben. Da man im Lateinischen „viele" mit „multi" übersetzt, kann man also getrost von einer multikulturellen Gesellschaft sprechen.
Was aber sichert den Zusammenhalt in einer multikulturellen Gesellschaft? Multikulturell heißt gerade nicht, dass jeder machen kann, was er will. Wenn in Deutschland

etwa im Namen einer Kultur Frauenrechte missachtet werden, muss im Namen des Grundgesetzes die Einhaltung des Rechts durchgesetzt werden.

Nein, es führt kein Weg vorbei an einer gemeinsamen Leitkultur, in der wir uns auf Grundwerte verständigen, die über das Grundgesetz hinaus Identität schaffen. Das heißt nicht, dass wir über unsere Grundrechte mit Islamisten verhandeln. Das Grundgesetz ist nicht verhandelbar. Doch welche Werte bilden den Kitt unserer Gesellschaft? Wie sollte eine solche Debatte geführt werden, damit sie nicht zerfranst, sondern einen Kanon von Werten schafft, den Deutsche und Zuwanderer akzeptieren? Diese Fragen bewegen uns in Nordrhein-Westfalen in besonderer Weise, denn von rund 18 Millionen Einwohnern haben etwa vier Millionen Menschen eine Zuwanderungsgeschichte.

Um zu einem brauchbaren Ergebnis zu kommen, ist es ratsam, in der Debatte davon auszugehen, was in unserer multikulturellen Gesellschaft allen gemein ist und was wir anstreben müssen, damit wir uns in Zukunft behaupten können. Daher könnte die zentrale Frage etwa so lauten: Wie schaffen wir in unserer heutigen Gesellschaft Bedingungen, die unsere im Arbeitsprozess stehenden und nachwachsenden Generationen in die Lage versetzen, sich im allgemeinen Wettbewerb in einer globalisierten Welt behaupten zu können - ungeachtet der geistigen Unterschiede, die die Kulturen trennen. Gewiss, eine gemeinsame Antwort auf diese Frage zu finden ist nicht leicht. Doch es ist möglich, wenn wir uns auf einige Voraussetzungen verständigen.

Erstens: Die Würde und die Gleichwertigkeit jedes einzelnen Menschen sind unantastbar. So will es das Grundgesetz, der Geist unserer Verfassung jedoch ist keineswegs überall in Deutschland gelebte Praxis. Die Herausforderung für Deutsche und Zuwanderer liegt darin, zu lernen, den anderen in seiner Existenz und in seinen Überzeugungen anzuerkennen und zu achten - ohne dass das eigene Selbstwertgefühl und die Richtigkeit eigener Überzeugungen infrage gestellt werden. Denn Respekt und Akzeptanz des Fremden setzen die Wertschätzung des eigenen Ichs voraus. Doch haben wir Deutsche das in ausreichendem Maße? Mein Eindruck ist, dass wir uns wieder klar darüber werden müssen, dass unsere Ansprüche an eine offene Gesellschaft nur Zukunft haben werden, wenn auch die sie formenden kulturellen Überzeugungen in ihnen lebendig bleiben.

Die Muslime dagegen müssen, und das wäre mein zweiter Punkt, die in unserer Kultur gewachsene Trennung von Religion und Staat akzeptieren. Es ist sicher nicht Sache westlicher Staaten, den Islam zu reformieren, aber man kann zu Recht verlangen, jene zum Schweigen zu bringen, die Hass auf den Westen und alle Nichtmuslime schüren.

Drittens: Es muss bei uns Deutschen die Bereitschaft wachsen, auf Mitbürger aus anderen Kulturen zuzugehen sowie Interesse für ihre Sitten, Gebräuche und Freizeitgestaltung zu zeigen. Wir müssen mehr Verständnis und Anerkennung zeigen für Menschen anderer Kulturen. Diese müssen sich ihrerseits ebenfalls um Zusammenarbeit mit uns und um Integration bemühen. So sollten Zuwanderer mehr Verständnis dafür entwickeln, dass ihre Kinder bessere Bildungschancen in Deutschland haben, wenn sie frühzeitig unsere gemeinsame Sprache lernen. Sie müssen erkennen, dass Ausgrenzung unserer gemeinsamen Zukunft und der ihrer Kinder schadet.

Das harmonische Zusammenleben der Generationen, Kinderfreundlichkeit, der Respekt vor älteren Menschen und die Achtung religiöser Überzeugungen sind dagegen Werte, die fest in der Lebenswelt der Zuwanderer verankert sind - von unserer Gesellschaft aber wieder neu entdeckt werden müssen. So käme wohl kein Zuwanderer auf die Idee, dass Kinder nach ihrem 25. Lebensjahr nicht mehr für ihre Eltern verantwortlich sind - so wie es bei der Reform des Hartz-IV-Gesetzes ernsthaft diskutiert wurde.

Auch zeigen Zuwanderer großen Respekt vor den religiösen Überzeugungen anderer – ein Wert, der bei uns verloren zu gehen droht. Müssen unsere Medien eigentlich jede Geschmacklosigkeit publizieren, die die Gefühle religiöser Menschen verletzt? Warum müssen sich gläubige Christen in unserem Land jeden medialen Schlag unter die Gürtellinie gefallen lassen? Ich begrüße den Protest der deutschen Katholiken gegen die TV-Serie *Popetown*.

Kurzum: Vorurteile müssen auf beiden Seiten abgebaut werden. Doch dies gelingt uns nur, wenn mehr zwischenmenschliche Kontakte zwischen Muslimen, Christen und Nichtgläubigen in der Bevölkerung geknüpft werden. Deshalb muss die Debatte über gemeinsame Werte nicht zuvörderst in der Politik geführt werden – sondern in Vereinen, Verbänden und Schulen. Wir sollten schnell damit beginnen.

Armin Laschet: Von den Zuwanderern lernen. In: DIE ZEIT 24/2006

LÖSUNG: TRAININGSAUFGABE 12

Lösungsvorschlag

Aufgabe

Prepare the Minister's statement **in English** that reflects what he wrote in his article. The statement should focus on the four questions which have to be answered by him during the panel discussion in London.

HINWEIS   Bei dieser Aufgabe müssen Sie den Situationsbezug beachten. Es handelt sich um eine Stellungnahme des Integrationsministers von Nordrhein-Westfalen in der deutschen Botschaft in London. Dies gibt Ihnen auch einen Hinweis auf das erwartete hohe Sprachniveau. Außerdem muss die Übertragung des Textes die vier in der Aufgabenstellung vorgegebenen Leitfragen beantworten. Andere Aussagen können entsprechend knapper gehalten werden, sodass Ihre Lösung in etwa um die Hälfte kürzer ausfallen wird als der Originaltext.

Lösungsschritte

1. Lesen Sie den Text aufmerksam durch.
2. Lesen Sie die Aufgabenstellung, markieren Sie Situations- und Adressatenbezug und unterstreichen Sie Schlüsselwörter in der Aufgabenstellung, um Schwerpunkte und Redundanzen besser zu erkennen.
3. Lesen Sie den Text erneut und markieren Sie Schlüsselstellen.
4. Fertigen Sie Ihre Übertragung an und überlegen Sie während der Arbeit immer wieder, welche Inhalte wichtig sind. Fassen Sie Wiederholungen zusammen. Achten Sie auch auf Verständlichkeit und Logik. Überprüfen Sie die sinnvolle Verwendung von Konnektoren, angemessenen sprachlichen Strukturen und Vokabular.
5. Lesen Sie abschließend Ihre Übertragung noch einmal durch, wobei Sie den Bezug zur Aufgabenstellung überprüfen. Achten Sie auch auf Verständlichkeit und Logik sowie auf ein angemessenes sprachliches Niveau. Streichen Sie unter Umständen Redundanzen.

Ausführliche Lösung

Considering the fact that for decades more and more people from foreign countries have come to Germany in order to live there, it is unquestionable that Germany is a multicultural society. Multicultural does not mean that everyone can do whatever he or she wants to do: there must be an agreement among all residents and citizens of a country on basic common values and rules to create some common identity. A not negotiable set of laws is our constitution, the "Grundgesetz". Furthermore, a consensus on common values beyond the constitution must be created. This is especially important in areas like North-Rhine Westphalia where four out of 18 million inhabitants have an immigration background.

In order to cope with the challenges of the future as a nation, it is advisable to agree on common social aims. How to prepare our future generations for economic competition in a globalized world is one of the major issues that may represent a common basis. Not only due to cultural differences is it not easy but possible to find a solution if we agree on some premises:

First of all the idea that human dignity and equality are inviolable must be paramount everywhere in the country. Germans and immigrants have to learn to accept and respect every human being's existence and his or her convictions without fearing the loss of one's own identity and the belief in one's own views.

Secondly, immigrants must accept the separation of religion and state. Western states cannot reform Islam but they can stop those who fuel hatred against the West and non-Muslim states.

Thirdly, there must be mutual interest in each others' customs and way of life. Immigrants must strive for more cooperation and integration. They should accept that their children's opportunities are increased if they learn the language properly and that failure to integrate reduces their chances.

Family values and respect for the elderly and children are far more widespread among immigrants and must be rediscovered by our society. Immigrants also respect other religions far more than we do. Our media think nothing of insulting religious believers.

Prejudices have to be reduced on both sides. But this can only be achieved by mutual personal and social contacts among Muslims, Christians and atheists in our society. For that reason the discussion of common values must be held in associations, clubs and schools.

(393 words)

Notizen

Trainingsaufgabe 13

Aufgabentyp	Mediation
Thema	Immigration in the United Kingdom
Material	Nicola Jacobi: *Weit weg von Zuhause – Minderjährige Flüchtlinge in Deutschland.* www.goethe.de
Textsorte	Zeitungsartikel
Niveau	Grundkurs und Leistungskurs

Assignments

Imagine you are working as an intern for an English newspaper. It is your task to write an article about the situation of young foreigners in Germany, which focuses on the topic 'Dreams and Reality'.
Use the following prompts as a guideline for your article:

- What are reasons for and the circumstances of their migration?
- Which problems are they confronted with on arriving in Germany? Describe their living conditions.

Write this newspaper article, in which you summarise the main points of the text and pay special attention to the key questions above.

Material

Nicola Jacobi
Weit weg von Zuhause – Minderjährige Flüchtlinge in Deutschland

Zweimal pro Woche geht William zum Fußballtraining in München. Später würde er gerne für einen der großen Vereine kicken – Träume von einem anderen Leben. Denn William stammt aus Sierra Leone, einem Land, das sich nur langsam erholt von einem über zehn Jahre dauernden Bürgerkrieg. Vor einem Jahr kam er als Flüchtling nach
5 Deutschland, 17 Jahre alt, alleine, ohne Eltern oder Verwandte. Warum er sein Zuhause verlassen hat, darüber will er nicht sprechen. Vielleicht aus Armut, vielleicht weil seine Eltern im Krieg getötet wurden, vielleicht, weil seine Familie ihn geschickt hat. Er ist einer von rund 2000 so genannten unbegleiteten minderjährigen Flüchtlingen, die jedes Jahr in Deutschland Asyl suchen.
10 Wie William blocken viele Flüchtlinge bei Fragen nach dem Grund ihrer Flucht ab. Es gibt auch Familien, die die Flucht für ihre Kinder organisieren, in der Hoffnung, dass wenigstens eines überlebt. Zwischen 6000 und 10000 unbegleitete minderjährige Flüchtlinge leben in Deutschland, so schätzt der Verband. Genaue Zahlen gibt es nicht, denn UMF, wie sie auch genannt werden, sind nirgendwo statistisch erfasst.
15 Auch wie sie nach Deutschland kommen, verraten sie oft nur bruchstückhaft. William erzählt, er sei mit dem Flugzeug gekommen, ein Mann hätte ihn in den Zug begleitet, sei aber irgendwo auf der Strecke ausgestiegen. So landete er in München. Er irrte

umher, fragte andere Afrikaner um Hilfe, schließlich kam ein Deutscher auf ihn zu und brachte ihn zu einem Asylheim. Manche Flüchtlingskinder haben Bekannte, die bereits in Deutschland leben. „Aber es gibt auch viele Neuankömmlinge, die gar nicht wissen, an welche Stellen sie sich wenden müssen. Die Polizei greift sie dann irgendwo auf", sagt Albert Riedelsheimer, Vorsitzender des Bundesfachverbandes Unbegleitete Minderjährige Flüchtlinge in Nürnberg. „Illegal bleiben nur sehr wenige. Erstens ist die Wahrscheinlichkeit groß, dass sie irgendwo kontrolliert werden, zweitens brauchen sie offizielle Dokumente, wenn sie in die Schule oder zum Arzt gehen wollen." Einen Pass besitzen nur die wenigsten. Also wird das Alter bei den Behörden geschätzt - nach Inaugenscheinnahme, wie es heißt. Einige der jungen Flüchtlinge versuchen, sich jünger zu machen als sie sind. Für Jugendliche unter 16 Jahren ist die Betreuung besser.

Oft landen 16- und 17-jährige Flüchtlinge in allgemeinen Asylunterkünften, von denen nur wenige Wohngruppen für Jugendliche mit spezieller Betreuung anbieten. William wohnt seit einigen Monaten in einer solchen Gruppe in München - in einer Container-Wohnanlage, in der insgesamt 200 Menschen leben. Die Jugendgruppe besteht aus 30 jungen Männern aus mehr als zehn verschiedenen Nationen, jeweils zwei aus dem gleichen Land teilen sich ein Zimmer. „Trotz der Enge funktioniert das Zusammenleben der Kulturen recht gut", sagt Bettina Pereira von der Caritas. Sie arbeitet seit mehr als sechs Jahren als Sozialpädagogin in der Unterkunft und betreut das Wohnprojekt. William denkt da anders, er hat außer zu seinem Zimmernachbarn kaum Kontakt. „Ich traue ihnen nicht", sagt er. „Es wird geklaut und die Leute halten die Räume nicht sauber. Es gibt keine Regeln." Doch solange er keinen sicheren Aufenthaltsstatus hat, muss er hier bleiben.

Trotz allem gefällt es ihm in München. Hier hat er zum ersten Mal Schnee gesehen. Er hofft, in Deutschland eine Ausbildung machen und arbeiten zu können. „Elektronik interessiert mich", sagt er. Aber noch lieber will er Fußballprofi werden.

Quelle: http://www.goethe.de
Autorin: Nicola Jacobi. Abdruck mit freundlicher Genehmigung des Goethe-Instituts (www.goethe.de)

Notizen

| MEDIATION

Lösungsvorschlag

Aufgabe

Write this newspaper article, in which you **summarise** the main points of the text and pay special attention to the key questions above.

HINWEIS Hier müssen Sie einen Zeitungsartikel schreiben, der die Situation junger Ausländer in Deutschland zusammenfasst. Leitfragen geben Ihnen eine Richtlinie, wie Sie Schwerpunkte setzen sollen. Dabei ist zu beachten, dass der Textteil über William in der Fragestellung nicht erwähnt ist. Daher können Sie ihn auch bei der Übertragung vernachlässigen, was die Mediation entsprechend verkürzt. Vergessen Sie nicht, sich eine passende Überschrift auszudenken.

Lösungsschritte

1. Lesen Sie den Text aufmerksam durch.
2. Lesen Sie die Aufgabenstellung, markieren Sie Situations- und Adressatenbezug und unterstreichen Sie Schlüsselwörter in der Aufgabenstellung, um Schwerpunkte und Redundanzen besser zu erkennen.
3. Lesen Sie den Text erneut und markieren Sie Schlüsselstellen.
4. Fertigen Sie Ihre Übertragung an und überlegen Sie während der Arbeit immer wieder, welche Inhalte wichtig sind. Fassen Sie Wiederholungen zusammen. Achten Sie auch auf Verständlichkeit und Logik. Überprüfen Sie die sinnvolle Verwendung von Konnektoren, angemessenen sprachlichen Strukturen und Vokabular.
5. Lesen Sie abschließend Ihre Übertragung noch einmal durch, wobei Sie den Bezug zur Aufgabenstellung überprüfen. Achten Sie auch auf Verständlichkeit und Logik sowie auf ein angemessenes sprachliches Niveau.

Ausführliche Lösung

Dreams and Reality

Every year about 2,000 underage refugees arrive in Germany. Between 6,000 and 10,000 young asylum seekers probably live in Germany now, but there are no reliable statistics.
The reasons for their escape are similar, e. g. civil wars and poverty in their home countries. Some of them are sent by their relatives in the hope of better living and working conditions for their children. The teenagers often do not reveal the circumstances of their journey to Germany, which often are very risky. Many of them are accompanied by professionals who take the children to their destination country. Others arrive by plane or have the advantage of being hosted by relatives or acquaintances.
When they reach Germany, they often do not know where to go first and roam around aimlessly. Some of them are caught by the police. As most of them do not possess a passport or legal documents, many pretend to be younger than they really are in order to get the additional support provided by the state to those under sixteen. Those without any connections in Germany often end up in an accommodation for asylum seekers, where they live in poor and confined circumstances. Although social workers claim that

the cohabitation of different cultures and ages works well, young asylum seekers complain about theft and a lack of tidiness in the buildings.
Only few remain illegal as they are controlled by the police and because they need legal documents to attend school or go to the doctor. Often the authorities must estimate the refugees' age.

(259 words)

Notizen

ANHANG

Formulierungshilfen und

Redewendungen

Formulierungshilfen und Redewendungen

Auf den folgenden Seiten finden Sie nützliche Formulierungen und Redewendungen, die Sie beim Abfassen Ihrer schriftlichen Abiturarbeit einsetzen können. Sortiert sind die Vorschläge nach den Arbeitsanweisungen, die Sie in den Aufgabenstellungen finden.

1. Analyse – analysieren

Beschreiben Sie bestimmte Aspekte oder Merkmale eines Textes und erklären Sie diese.

Die Einstellung des Autors analysieren/untersuchen:

The writer …
- attacks the idea that …
- doubts the evidence for …/that …
- questions the facts about …/the claim that …
- criticises the attitude of …
- pokes fun at …/ridicules the idea/suggestion that …
- gives a prejudiced/one-sided picture/view of …
- warns of a development that could/might …
- has a critical/objective/sceptical view of …
- has a/an approving/positive/disapproving/negative attitude towards …

Den Sprachgebrauch analysieren/untersuchen:

- The author makes use of colloquial/informal/formal language.
- The author's use of words and expressions like … and … shows …
- The author's use of … is a play on words as it can be understood to mean …
- The author's attitude to … is expressed by his use of language like …
- The author's use of stylistic devices such as … and … emphasises that.

2. Assess – beurteilen

Stellen Sie die Gründe für oder gegen etwas dar und beurteilen Sie diese möglichst ausgewogen.

- (to) assess a course of action/decision/policy/situation
- (to) assess the importance/significance of …
- (to) examine a decision/situation and pass judgement on it
- (to) make up one's mind about …
- (to) arrive at a (final) decision/position about/on …
- In/When assessing the problem/issue/question of …, it is necessary/useful to take the following factors into account before arriving at a final judgement/opinion. Firstly, …, secondly, …
- An assessment of … presupposes/requires an examination of a number of/several factors, namely …
- The author's/writer's assessment of … is quite different from my own. In my view, it is quite clear that …

FORMULIERUNGSHILFEN UND REDEWENDUNGEN 115

- I share the author's assessment of … in so far as/to the extent that …, but in my opinion he/she exaggerates/underestimates/places too much/little emphasis on …
- In arriving at a final judgement/opinion, I have placed a high value on …, which I consider/think to be decisive.

3. Characterise – charakterisieren

Hier sollen Sie die Charaktere beschreiben und untersuchen, wie sie präsentiert werden. Seien Sie vorsichtig im Bereich von negativen Merkmalen. Dabei werden oft Fehler gemacht, weil sie in anderem Kontext verwendet werden als im Deutschen.

Charakterisierung von Personen:

- (to) characterise a person directly/indirectly
- (to) describe a character/person/protagonist
- (to) get/receive information about/insights into a character's personality/state of mind
- (to) begin by telling the reader that …
- (to) transmit information about … by …
- (to) understand that … is a/an emotional/strong/weak/dishonest/hypocritical/… person because we are told/read/hear that …
- (to) interpret a character's actions as suggesting that …

Positive Charaktermerkmale:

agreeable (angenehm), cooperative, courageous, fair/fair-minded, generous, honest, loyal, nice, open, pleasant, predictable (berechenbar), reliable (zuverlässig), tolerant, trustworthy, understanding, warm-hearted, well-behaved …

Negative Charaktermerkmale:

aggressive, boastful (angeberisch), brutal, cold, cynical, disagreeable (unangenehm), disloyal, greedy, mean (gemein), narrow-/small-minded (engstirnig), nasty, pompous, promiscuous (den/die Sexualpartner/-in häufig wechselnd), sly (gerissen), unfair, unpleasant, unpredictable (unberechenbar), unreliable (unzuverlässig), violent, vulgar …

4. Compare – vergleichen

Ähnlichkeiten und Unterschiede sollen hier ermittelt und aufgezeigt werden.

- In comparison with …, … is/appears to be …
- When compared with …, … may be seen as/seems …
- A comparison between … and … suggests that …
- On the one hand, we gather/hear/read/understand that … is …, but on the other (hand) we also …
- In so far as … is …, the reader understands that he/she/it is …
- When comparing … with …, it is necessary/useful to note that …
- The author/writer points out the similarities/differences between … and …

ANHANG

- In explaining/pointing out the similarities/differences between ... and ..., the author/writer intends to express the idea that ...

5. Contrast – kontrastieren

Identifizieren Sie Unterschiede und stellen Sie diese dar.

- (to) contrast one opinion/position/view with another
- (to) draw up/point out the difference(s) between ... and ...
- (to) differentiate between ... and ...
- The contrast between ... and ... could hardly be greater/more marked.
- In contrast to ..., ... is/seems/may be said to be ...
- The author/writer draws a contrast between ... and ..., but this is flawed/misleading/mistaken/not the case. In my own opinion, the similarities are greater than the differences. For example, ...
- Any contrast between ... on the one hand, and ... on the other, must/should concentrate/focus on the issue/question of ...

6. Describe – beschreiben

Hier geht es um eine detaillierte und möglichst konkrete Darstellung von Abbildungen wie Fotos, Karikaturen usw.

Die Beschreibung von Cartoons:

- The cartoon/drawing/photo/picture illustrates/portrays/shows ...
- In the cartoon/drawing/..., we can identify/see/make out ...
- in the foreground/background/middle distance (nicht: "middleground"!)
- at the top/bottom
- in the middle; in the upper/lower half
- on the left/right; at the right/left side
- in the top right/left corner; in the bottom right/left corner
- the speech/thought bubble says "..."
- the caption says that/tells us that this is a photo/... of
- the artist uses a label/labels which says/say ...

7. Discuss – diskutieren

Untersuchen Sie ein Thema argumentativ mit Gründen dafür und dagegen.

Einleitung des Themas:

- It is important/useful to begin/open by saying/pointing out that ...
- It makes sense to start by asking whether ...
- There are a number of points/issues to consider here.
- There are several questions to think about when discussing ...
- The issues I want to mention/discuss here are ...
- In my opinion/view ...

- From my (own) point of view it is clear that ...
- Some may disagree, but I feel/think that ...

Auflistung erstellen:

- First, .../First of all, ...
- Secondly, .../Thirdly, ...
- Finally, .../Lastly, .../Last of all ...

Inhalte mit besonderer Betonung hinzufügen:

- In addition, ...
- Moreover, .../Furthermore, ...
- What is more, ...
- Not only ..., but ... also ...
- Another (important) point to consider is: ...
- A further point to emphasise/note ...
- It is often forgotten/overlooked that ...
- Even if that was not the case, we must not forget that ...

Alternativen und Gegensätze angeben:

- Alternatively, ...
- On the one hand, ... on the other (hand), ...
- However, .../Although .../Even though ...
- Despite (+ Gerundium)/In spite of (+ Gerundium)

Gründe und Ursachen definieren:

- Because .../Since ...
- The reason(s) for ... is/are that ...
- The reason why ... is that ...
- The cause(s) of this situation is/are ...

Ergebnisse und Auswirkungen definieren:

- As a result (of this), .../As a consequence (of this), ...
- The effect of this is that ...
- The (inevitable) result of this situation/state of affairs is that ...

Schluss:

- To sum up, ...
- In short, .../In general, ...
- On the whole, it can be said that ...
- In conclusion, then, it is clear that ...
- To conclude, therefore, it is hard to deny that ...

8. Evaluate – auswerten

Bilden Sie sich nach reiflicher Überlegung eine begründete Meinung und legen Sie diese dar.

- (to) evaluate a course of action/state of affairs
- (to) evaluate/weigh up the worth of …
- (to) examine a decision/situation
- (to) make up one's mind about …
- (to) form an opinion about/on …
- (to) get/receive an impression of …
- In/When evaluating the problem/question of …, it is necessary/useful to take the following factors into account. Firstly, …, secondly, …
- An evaluation of … requires that we enquire into/examine/look at a number of/several factors, namely …
- The author's evaluation of … is quite different from my own. In my view, …
- I share the author's evaluation of … in so far as/to the extent that …, but in my opinion he/she exaggerates/underestimates …

9. Explain – erklären

Im Gegensatz zur Beschreibung sollen Sie hier zusätzlich im Detail etwas definieren.

Die Erläuterung von grafischen Darstellungen:

- The line graph deals with/shows the relationship between productivity and labour costs in manufacturing industries between 1990 and 2005.
- The bar chart compares the pay of men and women in Sweden and the UK from 2000 to 2006.
- The pie chart deals with/shows the distribution of seats in the US Congress after the last election.
- The line rises gradually/slowly/sharply/steeply/fast and peaks at/reaches a peak at …
- The line falls gradually/slowly/sharply/steeply/fast and bottoms out at …
- The graph shows/illustrates a steady/sharp increase/rise/decrease/fall in street crime over the last two/… years/…
- The pie chart is divided into five segments showing the number of votes won by the five main parties in the federal election of 2005.
- The pie chart shows/makes clear the current distribution of jobs in manufacturing and service industries in the USA.
- The statistics present data about/on youth unemployment in the EU/… at the end of 2007.
- According to official/UN/… statistics, poverty is increasing in Africa/…
- The statistics on/relating to outsourcing to Central Europe/Asia suggest that …
- The data is statistically insignificant (statistisch unbedeutend) because it falls within a 2 % margin of error.
- The statistics/figures are misleading because they do not include/take account of/take into account absence through ill health/…

10. Illustrate – veranschaulichen

Erklären bzw. verdeutlichen Sie etwas anhand von Beispielen.

Gebrauch von Stilmitteln:

- (to) make use of a stylistic/literary device
- (to) employ/use hyperbole/repetition/… when describing/speaking of …
- (to) make use of a simile/… to describe …
- (to) use understatement/… as when the author says in line …/in lines … and …
- the author's use of repetition/… in line … makes his/her attitude clear to the reader
- the author's style is formal/colloquial as when he/she writes in lines … to … "…"
- the writer is highly critical of … as when he/she refers to/points out that …

Funktion von Stilmitteln:

- (to) emphasise/stress a point/an argument
- (to) highlight a key event/incident
- (to) make one's opinion/position/meaning clear to the reader
- (to) create a colourful/vivid impression by making use of … in lines …
- (to) make use of hyperbole/… for emphasis
- (to) use metaphorical language to make clear one's intention/meaning
- (to) sound friendly/confiding by using the language of everyday speech

11. Interpret – interpretieren

Arbeiten Sie die Bedeutung des Textes heraus.

- (to) interpret a cartoon/drama/novel/poem/short story/…
- (to) interpret an extract/a passage/a quotation/a scene from …
- (to) concentrate/focus on …
- (to) emphasise/highlight/stress …
- (to) clarify/make clear/illuminate/shed light on
- (to) understand/take to mean
- (to) assume/read … into …
- The apparent meaning of this event/incident is …, but its submerged meaning is/may be taken/understood to be …

Interpretation des Sprachgebrauchs:

- (to) examine/investigate an author's use of imagery/symbolism, for example …
- (to) look at an author's use of language/style
- (to) explore a writer's use of literary/stylistic devices
- (to) represent/symbolise/stand for …
- The author's/writer's choice of words/style is formal/informal/colloquial as when he/she says …
- The author's/writer's use of language/choice of words indicates to the reader that he/she …

Interpretation der Einstellung des Autors:

The author/writer …
- attacks the idea that …
- doubts the evidence for …/that …
- criticises the attitude of …
- questions the facts about …
- pokes fun at/ridicules the claim/idea that …/of (+ Gerundium!)
- speaks in an exaggerated/inflated way about …
- gives/presents a biased/prejudiced/one-sided picture/view of …
- warns of a development that might/could …
- defends the argument that …
- is convinced of the fact that …
- has a (highly) emotional/judgemental/personal/subjective attitude towards …
- seems to have a balanced/impersonal/neutral/objective attitude towards …
- has a critical/sceptical view of …
- has an approving/disapproving opinion of …
- When he/she says "…", the writer is being ironical/sceptical/…
- His/Her view/attitude is prejudiced/… because he/she says "…"

12. Justify – rechtfertigen

Präsentieren Sie ausreichende Gründe für Entscheidungen oder Schlussfolgerungen.

- (to) give grounds/reasons for a course of action/a decision/a point of view
- (to) give a justification for …
- (to) give/present an explanation of …
- (to) demonstrate/show/prove that a course of action/decision/opinion/situation is justified/reasonable/sensible
- The author/writer justifies his/her opinion/position on the grounds that …
- The government/… justifies its decision/policy on two/three/… grounds, namely …
- I agree with the author's/writer's argument that … is justified in so far as …
- The justification for this policy/… is said to be …, but this is clearly not the case. To begin with, it is undeniable that …
- On the contrary, common sense/experience/natural justice suggests that … is the case.
- The author's/writer's position is less a justification than an excuse (Ausrede).
- The fact (of the matter) is …

13. Outline – umreißen

Präsentieren Sie nur die Schwerpunkte eines Themas, ohne zu sehr ins Detail zu gehen.

- The author's/writer's main/most important/principal arguments are …
- In outline, the author's/… point is that …
- Without going into detail, the text makes clear that …
- Turning to the effects of globalisation/…, the writer's main point is …
- As far as globalisation/… is concerned, the writer focuses on …

14. Point out – hinweisen auf

Filtern Sie bestimmte Aspekte eines Themas heraus und erklären Sie diese.

The author/writer/journalist/reporter …
- describes the situation of …
- informs the reader about …
- tries to persuade the reader to …
- tells the reader how to … most effectively/easily
- explains the situation of …/the sequence of events leading to …
- attacks the idea that …
- doubts the evidence for …/that …
- criticises the attitude of …
- questions the facts about …
- gives a biased/one-sided view of …
- warns of the possibility/likelihood that …/of …
- defends the argument that …
- tries to be objective about …
- seems to have a neutral/balanced attitude towards …

15. Summarise – zusammenfassen

Geben Sie eine kurze Darstellung der Schwerpunkte eines Textes und vermeiden Sie unnötige Details und Nebensächlichkeiten. Hier sind Schlüsselwörter aus dem Text eine wichtige Hilfe; sie verweisen auf die Hauptinformationen des Textes. Die Fragewörter *wer*, *was*, *wo*, *wann*, *wie* und *warum* können Ihnen helfen, die Schlüsselwörter zu erkennen. Benutzen Sie Aufzählungen und Konjunktionen, um eine Zusammenfassung zu strukturieren und um Sätze und Absätze miteinander zu verbinden.

- firstly/secondly/…; to begin with
- then; after that; goes on to say/emphasise/…
- finally/(nicht: at/in the end); in conclusion
- although; moreover, furthermore; …
- on the one hand …, but on the other (hand) …
- either … or …; neither … nor …
- despite/in spite of this; nevertheless; …

False Friends

Hier ist eine Liste von „falschen Freunden", die Sie oft und gerne im Stich lassen. In der linken Spalte steht das deutsche Wort. In der mittleren Spalte finden Sie die richtige englische Entsprechung im Kontext. Rechts steht der typische Fehler.

Verben

bemerken	I'm sorry. I didn't **notice** you.	~~remark~~
irritieren	Don't **distract** Ann. She's counting.	~~irritate~~
meinen	Tom **thinks** Sally is fantastic.	~~means~~
machen	Have you **done** your homework yet?	~~made~~
spenden	Germans **donate** a lot of money to charity.	~~spent~~
starten	The plane **took off** two hours late.	~~started~~
übersehen	The driver **overlooked** a red light.	~~oversaws~~

Nomen

Land	Bavaria is the biggest **state** in Germany.	~~land~~
Menü	The **set meal** costs $4.50.	~~menu~~
Pension	**Guest houses** are cheaper than hotels.	~~pension~~
Politik	The government's rail **policy** is crazy.	~~politic(s)~~
Preis	Our school won a **prize** of £1000.	~~price~~
Rente	I can't live on such a small **pension**.	~~rent~~
Rezept	Take this **prescription** to the chemist's.	~~recipe~~

Adjektive, Adverbien

aktuell	Global warming is a **current** problem.	~~actual~~
brav	I'm afraid Bonzo isn't very **well-behaved**.	~~brave~~
dezent	Please wear **discreet/subdued** clothing.	~~decent~~
desinteressiert	John's **uninterested** in school.	~~disinterested~~
dick	The doctor said I'm too **fat**.	~~thick~~
eventuell	**Maybe** we'll call in at the weekend.	~~eventually~~
komfortabel	They live in a **luxurious** flat in Berlin.	~~comfortable~~
miserabel	This steak is absolutely **awful**.	~~miserable~~
nächste	The **nearest** post office is in Cherry Road.	~~next~~
neueste	Is this the **latest** version of Word?	~~newest~~
sensibel	Jim's very **sensitive** about his big feet.	~~sensible~~
seriös	We only do business with **reputable** firms.	~~serious~~
sympathisch	Mrs Todd is a **likeable** woman.	~~sympathetic~~

ORIGINALPRÜFUNG 2012
Grundkurs

PRÜFUNGSAUFGABEN 2012

Vorschlag A: The Electronic Dream

Assignments

1. Summarize the text. (Material) (30 BE)
2. Compare the influence of innovative technology on everyday life to the influence of innovative technology on life in a utopian/dystopian society dealt with in class. Take the text at hand as a starting-point. (40 BE)
3. "But, in fact, is it true that the happiness of the individual advances as man advances? Nothing is more doubtful" (Emile Durkheim, 1893).
   Discuss the problem raised by Durkheim, taking the text at hand as a starting point. (30 BE)

Material

From tips to clicks: restaurants try e-menus
By Rebecca Harrison, TEL AVIV (Reuters) – Enter the e-waiter, Monday, Feb 25, 2008

Restaurants in Europe, the United States, and Japan are testing technology to let diners order their food directly from a screen at their table instead of depending on a fellow human being to note their choice – sometimes grumpily[1] or erroneously[2].
Besides cutting costs, companies that sell the "e-menu" argue the bytes-for-bites approach has
5 a novelty value that can lure younger customers and boost revenues as tantalising[3] photographs of succulent[4] steaks and gooey[5] desserts tempt diners to order more.
It also could extend the TV dinner. How about a computer-game dinner?
The idea may be only the latest gimmick[6] in a trade which is driven by consumer appetites and where fads[7] help. But at least for now, it appears to be boosting business.
10 In Israel, privately owned start-up Conceptic has already installed e-menu technology in sushi bars, pubs, and family restaurants. The system is based on touch screens already used in self-service canteens or for ticketing in airports and cinemas.
"It's about impulse-buying," said Adi Chitayat, Conceptic's chief executive. "If a person starts looking at pictures of chocolate cake, the chances are he'll order it." [...]
15 Frame, a trendy sushi restaurant in Tel Aviv, Israel, which has installed the system, said sales on tables with the e-menu have increased by about 11 percent. Customers often call ahead to reserve spots equipped with the screens, manager Natalie Edry told Reuters.
At one of the e-menu tables, information technology worker Gil Uriel and his young family were enthusiastic as they checked out pictures of the dishes on offer and squabbled over
20 desserts.
"It's more visual," said Uriel, as his children clicked away furiously on a games function between courses. "We can still choose, we can still argue – but it's much easier when you can all see it." [...]
Microsoft says its new Microsoft Surface system, which transforms an entire table into one big
25 touch screen, is due to go live in spring 2008 in some U.S. hotels and casinos, letting customers order food directly as well as play music and games.
The Seattle-based giant says on its Web site it will "transform the way people shop, dine, entertain, and live." Both Conceptic and Microsoft argue their examples of interactive and communal technology represent the future.
30 "We are living in a technology age," said Conceptic's Chitayat. "People are not afraid of screens." The company, which launched its pilot in 2006, expects to turn a profit in mid-2009, he added. [...]
Chitayat said taking computers into restaurants is an obvious next step after technology revo-

lutionized the workplace, although he noted restaurants with the e-menu – including Frame –
35 still rely on waiters to deliver the food. [...]
But many diners doubt the e-menu idea will take off.
"I don't believe in screens; I believe in humans," said businessman Yoash Torkman as he lunched at Frame. "I'll wait for 15 minutes for a waitress instead of using this. It's a gimmick and gimmicks have very short lives."
40 In Europe, where dining out is a time-honored tradition as much about good conversation and etiquette as staving off[8] hunger, waiting staff were unsurprisingly circumspect[9].
"See this man here? He's been coming here for 25 years," said a waitress at Italian restaurant Rosticceria Fiorentina in Brussels, who gave her name only as Giovanna. "I know his wife; I know his daughter. Do you think it would be better if he was welcomed by computer?" [...]
45 "There are always some people who embrace a new technology but others will avoid it for as long as possible," said Jackie Fenn, emerging technology analyst at Gartner consulting group. "Will a bunch of teenagers have a blast using it? Yes. But it will take time to move from being an attraction in a small number of restaurants to something that is widespread."

(622 words)

http://www.reuters.com/article/idUSL204599320080225 [zuletzt aufgerufen am 14.05.2012]

1 grumpily – mürrisch
2 erroneously – irrtümlich
3 tantalising – extremely tempting
4 succulent – juicy
5 gooey – sweet and sticky
6 gimmick – Masche, Trick
7 fads – Modeerscheinungen
8 stave off – vermeiden von, abwehren
9 circumspect – vorsichtig/zurückhaltend

Vorschlag B: Multiculturalism

Assignments

1   Summarize the article. (Material) (30 BE)
2   Relate Canada's approach to multiculturalism to the situation in either the USA or Great Britain. Refer to material discussed in class. (40 BE)
3   "Is wanting to preserve your country's cultural identity a bad thing?"
    http://www.sherdog.net/forums/f54/wanting-preserve-you-countrys-cultural-identity-bad-thing-1173076/index3.html [zuletzt aufgerufen am 14.05.2012]

    Discuss. (30 BE)

Material

Multiculturalism has been Canada's solution, not its problem
by Irene Bloemraad, The Globe and Mail, October 28, 2010

German Chancellor Angela Merkel recently made headlines when she pronounced multiculturalism in Germany a failure. Shortly before, a Globe and Mail editorial argued that Canadians should eradicate "multiculturalism" from their vocabulary and refocus on "citizenship." Multiculturalism isn't just out of style, these statements suggest – it's dangerous for building
5 unity in increasingly diverse societies.
Unfortunately, both analyses are dead wrong.
Social scientists can measure multiculturalism in a given society by examining the number and content of public policies and government pronouncements around cultural recognition and accommodation. Such indices show that Germany is not, and has never been, a multicul-
10 tural society.
Multiculturalism can't have failed in Germany because it was never tried. Turkish guest workers and other immigrants were never welcomed as future citizens – only as temporary labour. If Germans are now concerned about the consequences, the blame certainly doesn't lie with multiculturalism.
15 These indices also group countries such as France and Norway with Germany as least multicultural, Sweden, the Netherlands and the United States as moderately multicultural, and Australia and Canada as most multicultural.
Have Canada's past practices and policies hurt attempts to forge common citizenship out of diversity?
20 Absolutely not. Consider how many immigrants become citizens. The least multicultural countries count the lowest levels of citizenship; the moderate multicultural countries have somewhat more. In comparison, an overwhelming majority of immigrants proudly take up citizenship in Canada and Australia, the two countries that went furthest in the multicultural experiment.
25 The positive link between multiculturalism and citizenship is further supported by comparing Canadian policy with that of the United States. In 1971, the Canadian government began promoting a multiculturalism-based integration policy, which was enshrined[1] in the Charter of Rights and Freedoms in 1982 and expanded in 1988, when the Multiculturalism Act[2] became federal law. Over this same period, the U.S. enacted no formal immigrant integration program
30 or multiculturalism policy.
In 1970, in both Canada and the U.S., about 60 per cent of foreign-born residents had acquired citizenship. By 2006, the American Community Survey estimated that, of the 37.5 million foreign-born people living in the U.S., just 42 per cent were naturalized[3] citizens. By that same year, 73 per cent of immigrants to Canada had acquired citizenship, one of the highest rates in
35 the world.
ere are, of course, many possible explanations for this statistical gulf, but here are some factors that did *not* play a predominant role: different immigrant streams; the large undocumented

population in the U.S.; different costs and benefits of citizenship; easier or faster processing in Canada.

40 My research points to multiculturalism as a key factor driving Canada's success at citizenship integration. It legitimates diversity, provides a sense of inclusion and, through the multitude of (oft-maligned[4]) government grants given to community-based organizations – not only for multiculturalism but also for a host of integration programs – it provides the support structures to help newcomers join the country as full citizens.

45 Canadians certainly can, and should, have thoughtful debates about recognizing and accommodating diversity – just as we debate health-care policy or Stanley Cup[5] contenders.

Like health care and hockey, multiculturalism has become a symbol of what defines Canada. In poll after poll, Canadians say multiculturalism is one of the top three defining features of the country. What's more, they are proud of it.

50 They should be. Over four decades, incredibly rapid demographic change has transformed Canada, especially its largest cities. In Europe, similar change has resulted in riots and cultural tensions that have tarnished[6] the concept of multiculturalism there. But, in Canada, these changes, despite many challenges, happened peacefully, productively and positively. Multiculturalism was part of the solution, not the problem.

(641 words)

http://www.theglobeandmail.com/news/opinions/opinion/multiculturalism-has-been-canadas-solution-not-its-problem/article1775471/ [zuletzt aufgerufen am 14.05.2012]
© Irene Bloemraad

1 enshrined – niedergelegt
2 Multiculturalism Act – the act acknowledged the right of ethnic groups in Canada to preserve and share their unique cultural heritage; it also guaranteed equal opportunity for Canadians of all origins. This act has remained largely unchanged since 1988 with the exception of some minor amendments.
3 naturalized – eingebürgert
4 maligned – schlechtgemacht
5 Stanley Cup – North American hockey championship
6 tarnish – mit einem Makel versehen

Vorschlag C: Environment / Attitudes towards Work

Teil A: Aufgabe zur Sprachmittlung

Assignment

A group of environmental activists in Louisiana is interested in international opinions on U. S. environmental policies after the oil spill disaster in the Gulf of Mexico in 2010.

Summarize the excerpt for them. (Material A)

Teil B: Verkürzte Textaufgabe

Assignments

1	Describe the situation. (Material B)	(30 BE)
2	Compare Fatima's attitude to that of immigrants to the United States discussed in class. Refer to material discussed in class.	(40 BE)
3	Discuss how important money is for you when choosing your job. Take the text at hand as your starting point.	(30 BE)

Material A: Aufgabe zur Sprachmittlung

Öl – war da was?
Bislang haben wir bei jeder Umweltkatastrophe dazugelernt. Diesmal nicht.
von Andrea Böhm, 22. 7. 2010

Die Empörung über die Umweltkatastrophe ist grenzenlos. Protestaktionen gegen Ölfirmen im ganzen Land, in Kalifornien verbrennen Bürger ihre Kreditkarten, mit denen sie an Tankstellen Rabatt bekommen. Der Kongress handelt, der amerikanische Präsident unterzeichnet mehrere radikale Gesetze zum Umweltschutz.

5 Barack Obama im Jahr 2010? Nein, Richard Nixon[1] im Jahr 1970.
Auch damals ging es um eine Ölkatastrophe (und um verseuchte Flüsse). Das Fernsehen zeigte Bilder von toten Seevögeln, stillgelegten Fischereiflotten[2] und ölverschmierten Stränden – in diesem Fall lagen sie in Kalifornien[3]. Aber die politischen Zeiten waren offensichtlich andere. Vor vierzig Jahren zog der Schock über die ökologischen Folgen des Energiehungers politisches
10 Handeln nach sich, um ebendiese Folgen zu korrigieren. Und er beschleunigte den Aufstieg der amerikanischen Öko-Bewegung.
Erst kommt die Katastrophe, dann der Lernprozess, dann die Politik. Dieser Dreisatz prägte bislang die Geschichte des Umweltschutzes. Bislang. Angesichts des Desasters im Golf von Mexiko, verursacht durch die BP-Ölplattform *Deepwater Horizon,* zeigt sich der Staat ebenso
15 hilflos wie die Austernfischer[4] in Louisiana. Politischen Aufwind verspüren in den USA offenbar nicht die Befürworter neuer Auflagen zum Schutz von Natur und Klima, sondern deren Gegner. [...]
Mit der Verhängung eines vorläufigen Bohrstopps scheiterte Barack Obama an der amerikanischen Justiz und an der öffentlichen Meinung. Sein Appell an seine Landsleute, unter dem
20 Eindruck der Katastrophe eine neue, nachhaltige Energiepolitik zur nationalen Mission zu machen, verhallte.
Das Paradoxe dabei ist: Wir – denn es geht ja nicht nur um die Amerikaner – ertrinken bei der Berichterstattung über solche Katastrophen inzwischen in absurden wie erschreckenden Informationen über unser eigenes Zerstörungspotenzial. [...]
25 Wir wissen, dass die über 700 Millionen Liter Rohöl, die in den vergangenen Wochen in den Golf geflossen sind, etwa einem Fünftel des täglichen Verbrauchs der USA entsprechen. Wir haben außerdem gelernt, dass *oil spills* andernorts seit Jahrzehnten zur Tagesordnung gehören. [...]

Nur will der Lernprozess, also die Umsetzung dieser Informationen in politisches Handeln, heute nicht mehr so recht gelingen – nicht in den USA, nicht im Rest der Welt. [...]
Womöglich folgt die heilsame Wirkung des Schocks über *Deepwater Horizon* ja noch. Womöglich wird irgendwann eine überfällige Konvention ausgehandelt, eine Diskussion über ein Moratorium für Tiefseebohrungen[5] angeschoben und die Debatte über Klimaschutz aus dem Keller geholt. Aber vorerst ist keiner in Sicht, der den Anfang machen will oder kann. Barack Obama schon gar nicht. Der muss im November bei den Kongresswahlen mit einer verheerenden Niederlage rechnen.

(381 Wörter)

Die Zeit, 22. Juli 2010, Nr. 30, S. 8, http://www.zeit.de/2010/30/Umweltkatastrophe-Oelfirmen-Klimadebatte [zuletzt aufgerufen am 14.05.2012]

1   Richard M. Nixon – 37th President of the United States, 1969 – 1974
2   Fischereiflotte – fishing fleet
3   This refers to a major oil spill off Santa Barbara, CA, in January 1969
4   Austernfischer – oyster farmer
5   Tiefseebohrung – deep-sea drilling

Material B: Verkürzte Textaufgabe

Dashed Hopes

M. G. Vassanji's novel portrays the Lalani family, who are East-Indian immigrants to Canada, now living in the run-down apartment block 69 in Toronto's Don Mills district. The following excerpt describes a decisive moment for their daughter Fatima.

Fatima Lalani was standing squeezed into an elevator on her way up to receive the tidings[6] which she did not as yet know were bad. Her mother Zera had phoned her at the drugstore, where she worked after school, to tell her "it" had arrived, meaning the long-awaited letter from the university, and Fatima took off. In the elevator, although she greeted two small boys and threw a brief but disdainful glare at some of the more ordinary-looking people returning from work bearing parcels of groceries, she was as nervous as she had ever been in her life. It seemed to her that when she opened the envelope which was waiting for her, her entire life would be decided. It did not occur to her that the decision she awaited had already been made a few days before, and she whispered a prayer in much the same way her mother sometimes did; although she had never believed in, in fact had begun to scoff at[7] the efficacy[8] of this remedy, and her mother was the last role model she had in mind. [...]
When the elevator stopped on her floor, [...] Fatima could push herself out. Then, with a swing of her shoulders and a shake of her head, as if to banish the odours of cheap perfume and sweat and groceries, she strode off to her apartment. When she let herself in, her mother was waiting like an attendant, envelope in hand. Fatima grabbed it, tore it open, quickly read the gist, and slumped down on the sofa with a loud groan.
"What's it?" asked Zera, her mother, having guessed the answer.
"Arts and Science[9]," spoke Fatima in a mixture of grief and anger tinged with[10] drama.
"So? This is the end of the world then? Arts and Science – what's wrong with it?"
Fatima sulked, picking up the telephone and cradling it in her lap. During the last year, whenever any well-wisher asked her what she wanted to "become", she had given one unequivocal[11] reply: "Become rich." To many of the girls and boys of Sixty-nine and Sixty-seven and the other high-rise apartment buildings in this part of Don Mills, this is what growing up meant – making it. To the brighter ones, those with averages in the eighties and nineties[12], making it meant going to university: not to study pure science or humanities, but something more tangible[13], with "scope"[14], computer science or pharmacy for instance. For the girls, the latter of the two was preferable. It was more feminine, less threatening to the boys. Among the brighter girls of Don Mills the competition for a place to study pharmacy at the university is intense. Fatima Lalani, with an average of eighty-six, had struck out.
To Zera Lalani, of the old school, any education was a way out, a way up, and her daughter's

disappointment carried no significance beyond her having to put up with a bout of adolescent sulkiness.

(490 words)

Moyez G. Vassanji, No New Land, Toronto 1991, pp. 3 – 5

- 6   tidings – news
- 7   scoff at – make fun of
- 8   efficacy – Wirksamkeit
- 9   Arts and Science – Geistes- und Sozialwissenschaften
- 10 tinged with – mixed with
- 11 unequivocal – unmissverständlich
- 12 averages in the eighties and nineties – Ergebnisse gemessen im 100-Punkte-System; entspricht in etwa guten bis sehr guten Ergebnissen im deutschen System
- 13 tangible – handfest
- 14 scope – Entfaltungsmöglichkeit

LÖSUNGSVORSCHLAG 2012

Vorschlag A: The Electronic Dream

1 Summarize the text.

> **HINWEIS** Diese Aufgabe gehört zum Anforderungsbereich I. Sie sollen die wichtigsten Informationen des Textes effizient zusammenfassen (Operator *summarize*). Denken Sie daran, einen Einleitungssatz zu formulieren und die Präsenszeitformen zu verwenden.

Lösungsschritte zu Aufgabe 1

1	Lesen Sie den Text und markieren Sie wichtige Aussagen entsprechend der Aufgabenstellung.
2	Schreiben Sie einen Einleitungssatz (Autor, Titel des Textes, Textsorte, Quelle, Thema).
3	Formulieren Sie Ihre Zusammenfassung, achten Sie dabei auf Überleitungen.

> **HINWEIS** Verwenden Sie keine Zitate aus dem Originaltext und fügen Sie keine eigenen Kommentare ein.

Stichpunktlösung zu Aufgabe 1

- introductory sentence: online newspaper article "From tips to clicks: restaurants try e-menus" written by Rebecca Harrison, published on www.reuters.com, February 25, 2008, deals with the influence of modern technology on everyday life
- restaurants in various parts of the world have introduced ordering food online instead of from waitstaff
- attitudes to this innovation differ
- restaurants and developers tout its advantages, for example avoiding human error and surliness, reducing costs, attracting a younger clientele
- innovation appears very successful as sales have increased; customers tend to order more after having seen pictures of the food
- Microsoft has even extended the innovation to provide entertainment at the same time
- but system still depends on waiters serving the food
- innovation has opponents too
- claims of opponents: innovation is only a gimmick, personal contact with customers creates bonds, traditional dining also includes conversation and attention provided by well-trained waitstaff

2 Compare the influence of innovative technology ...

> **HINWEIS** Diese Aufgabe gehört zu den Anforderungsbereichen II und III. Sie sollen, ausgehend vom vorliegenden Text, den Einfluss neuer Technologien auf das Alltagsleben mit dem Einfluss neuer Technologien in einer utopischen oder einer dystopischen Gesellschaft vergleichen (Operator *compare*). Dazu muss Vorwissen aus dem Unterricht reaktiviert werden.

Lösungsschritte zu Aufgabe 2

1	Lesen Sie den Text und markieren Sie relevante Textstellen. Reaktivieren Sie Ihr Vorwissen aus dem Kurs zu folgenden Themen: a) neue Technologien im Alltag b) neue Technologien in utopischen/dystopischen Gesellschaften

Vorschlag A ■ LÖSUNGSVORSCHLAG 2012

2	Erarbeiten Sie eine Struktur:
	■ Einleitung: Ausgangspunkt - elektronische Bestellungen in Restaurants (Text)
	■ Hauptteil:
	   a) Einfluss innovativer Technologien auf das Alltagsleben
	   b) Vergleich mit dem Einfluss dieser Technologien in einer utopischen oder dystopischen Gesellschaft
	■ Schlussteil: Schlussfolgerung/Wertung/eigene Meinung/Ausblick auf die Zukunft

3	Formulieren Sie einen Text, achten Sie dabei auf Überleitungen zwischen den einzelnen Textabschnitten.
4	Prüfen Sie Ihren Text kritisch hinsichtlich Rechtschreibung, Grammatik und Ausdruck.

Stichpunktlösung zu Aufgabe 2

Introduction:
- typical example of an innovation that makes life more comfortable
- innovation introduces an additional aspect of automation to restaurants; in fast-food chains, automation has long simplified workers' tasks and improved choice and service for customers

Body:
- **a)** innovations to make life easier/more comfortable include *household devices* like washing machines, refrigerators, irons, *means of communication* like mobile phones, fax machines, PCs, *means of transportation* like trains, cars, planes
  - result of these innovations: freedom from time-consuming activities, leaving more time for studies/research or leisure activities
  - for women, innovations were the basis for emancipation as time-consuming household activities were taken over by household appliances → freedom to work, earn money, become independent
  - means of transportation: increase in trade, basis for globalization
  - means of communication: interconnection of different parts of the world – "global village", increase in trade/globalization, political/social interconnection, social networks
- **b)** examples of dystopian societies: *Fahrenheit 451* (R. Bradbury), *I, Robot* (I. Asimov), *1984* (G. Orwell), *Brave New World* (A. Huxley), *Oryx and Crake* (M. Atwood)
  - examples of utopian societies: *Ecotopia* (E. Callenbach), *Player Piano* (K. Vonnegut), *Looking Backward* (E. Bellamy)
  - innovative technologies continue to be developed and might anticipate possible future effects of social, economic, political development within a society in a positive or negative way
  - technologies might have inspirational/motivating/warning functions
  - these innovations might respond to certain social, political or technological needs within a society and anticipate their effects so that one might reconsider a possible development from a different perspective
  - these technologies might function as a basis for a possible political/economic/social development
  - example: *Fahrenheit 451* – total reliance of human beings on technology (esp. TV) estranges people from themselves, total absorption in technology leads to loss of human qualities (here: emotions, reading as basis for thinking)

Conclusion:
- innovative technologies make life more comfortable but might also bring disadvantages as people might become dependent on technology
- might deprive a customer ordering from an e-menu of the social contact with a waiter, thus cutting him off from the basis of society, i.e. social connection to other people

> **HINWEIS** Beziehen Sie sich im Hauptteil auf eine der im Lösungsvorschlag aufgeführten utopischen oder dystopischen Gesellschaften.

3 "But, in fact, is it true ..." Discuss the problem ...

> **HINWEIS** Diese Aufgabe gehört zum Anforderungsbereich III. Hier sollen Sie das im Zitat angesprochene Problem diskutieren (Operator *discuss*). Achten Sie darauf, das Zitat zu erläutern, den vorgegebenen Text als Ausgangspunkt zu verwenden, Pro- und Kontra-Aspekte des Problems gegenüberzustellen und daraus eine fundierte Schlussfolgerung zu ziehen.

Lösungsschritte zu Aufgabe 3

1	Lesen Sie den Text und unterstreichen Sie für die Diskussion notwendige Textstellen.

2	Sammeln Sie Material für den zu erstellenden Text (z. B. in Form einer Mindmap) und strukturieren Sie dieses sinnvoll:
	■ Einleitung: Bezug zum vorgegebenen Text
	■ Hauptteil:
	  a) Zitat erläutern
	  b) Pro-Argumente
	  c) Kontra-Argumente
	■ Schlussteil: Abwägen der Argumente/eigene Meinung/Rückbezug auf vorgegebenes Problem

3	Formulieren Sie Ihre Antwort und überprüfen Sie diese sprachlich (Grammatik, Rechtschreibung, Ausdruck).

Stichpunktlösung zu Aufgabe 3

Introduction:
- innovations meant to be beneficial to humans: make life easier or avoid unnecessary work, as text at hand shows
- e-menus are meant to offer a wider choice of food, improved service and entertainment at the same time

Body:
- **a)** quote questions the assumption that individual satisfaction increases with the advance of mankind, which in this context means technological progress
- **b)** arguments in favour of increased individual satisfaction:
  - development of machines like the Spinning Jenny (19th century): eased the lives of workers, beginning of Industrial Revolution, increased profits for individual factory owners, but also increased exploitation of workers
  - development of conveyor belt: made production cheaper, many individuals could afford products at low prices (example: Henry Ford's Model T), it increased profits of factory owners, but it also increased exploitation of individuals, reduced individual to being part of the machine
  - development of household appliances *(see task 2)*
  - outsourcing of production to China/India: low production costs mean low consumer prices (benefit for consumers in developed countries)
- **c)** arguments against increased human satisfaction:
  - advance of military development (example: development of atomic bomb): obviously no advance for the individuals suffering from the effects even today; aim: total destruction of individuals
  - advances in technology/outsourcing/reduction of production costs also include danger for the environment (example: production of jeans shown in documentary *China Blue*), high unemployment rates in developed countries, workers in China/India suffer from bad working conditions/long working hours
  - main aim: gain profit, not advance the well-being of humans

Conclusion:
- new technologies might always be regarded in two different ways: as beneficial or destructive to the individual
- benefits for many individuals often overruled by profit for a few
- question Durkheim raises is legitimate as it questions the value of each innovation for human progress
- asks reader to think about the necessity of innovations and warns that these could also reduce the existence of mankind to pure comfort/to an effortless life creating new dependencies

> **NÜTZLICHE WENDUNGEN** Die eigene Meinung äußern/stating one's opinion:
> - In my opinion/view ...
> - Personally, I believe that ...
> - Unlike ..., I find it hard to believe that ...
> - I would like to question the view that ...
> - ... is absolutely right in saying that ...
> - I share the view that ...
> - Considering all these arguments, ...
> - I would conclude that ...
> - I have come to the conclusion that ...

2012 LÖSUNGSVORSCHLAG ■ Vorschlag B

Vorschlag B: Multiculturalism

1 Summarize the article.

> HINWEIS Diese Aufgabe gehört zum Anforderungsbereich I. Sie sollen die wichtigsten Informationen des Textes kurz und knapp mit eigenen Worten wiedergeben (Operator *summarize*). Denken Sie daran, einen Einleitungssatz zu formulieren und die Präsenszeitformen zu verwenden.

Lösungsschritte zu Aufgabe 1

1	Lesen Sie den Text und markieren Sie wichtige Aussagen entsprechend der Aufgabenstellung.
2	Schreiben Sie einen Einleitungssatz (Autor, Titel des Textes, Textsorte, Quelle, Thema).
3	Formulieren Sie Ihre Zusammenfassung, achten Sie dabei auf Überleitungen.

> HINWEIS Verwenden Sie keine Zitate aus dem Originaltext und fügen Sie keine eigenen Kommentare ein.

Ausführlicher Lösungsvorschlag zu Aufgabe 1

The online newspaper article "Multiculturalism has been Canada's solution, not its problem" written by Irene Bloemraad, published in *The Globe and Mail* on October 28, 2010, deals with the approach to multiculturalism in different countries worldwide.

The author contrasts the different approaches, and states that in European countries, notably Germany, multiculturalism only appears to have failed; in reality, it never even existed. Bloemraad then ranks several countries with regard to their degree of multiculturalism.

Canada is deemed to be particularly multicultural; Bloemraad supports this claim with statistics and examples of relevant legislation. Canada has, for example, one of the world's highest numbers of immigrants who acquire citizenship. The author emphasizes the positive relationship between multiculturalism and citizenship immigration laws in recent years in Canada and the USA. She concludes that the strong Canadian integration policy has supported this high rate of citizenship acquisition, whereas the rate in the USA is rather low due to a complete lack of formal immigrant integration programs.

The author also names multiculturalism as the most important aspect of Canada's success in citizenship integration as it provides wide governmental and community-based support structures for the inclusion of newcomers. The result is that Canadians nowadays define multiculturalism as one of their country's key features. As Canada, in contrast to Europe, regards multiculturalism as the solution, not the problem, it benefits from positive changes within the country.

(229 words)

2 Relate Canada's approach to multiculturalism ...

> HINWEIS Diese Aufgabe gehört zu den Anforderungsbereichen II und III. Sie sollen, ausgehend vom vorliegenden Text, eine Verbindung zwischen Kanadas Umgang mit Multikulturalität zu der Situation in den USA oder in Großbritannien herstellen (Operator *relate*). Wichtig ist der Bezug zu dem aus dem Unterricht bekannten Material.

Lösungsschritte zu Aufgabe 2

1	Lesen Sie den Text und markieren Sie für die Aufgabenstellung relevante Textstellen.
2	Suchen Sie eine Vergleichssituation (USA/UK) und fertigen Sie Notizen an, strukturieren Sie diese und versehen Sie sie mit Beispielen aus Bezugstexten.

3	Strukturieren Sie Ihren Text:
	 ■ Einleitung
	 ■ Hauptteil:
	   a) Kanadas Umgang mit Multikulturalität
	   b) Vergleich mit USA/UK – Gemeinsamkeiten und Unterschiede
	 ■ Schlussteil: eigene Meinung/Ausblick auf die Zukunft

4	Formulieren Sie Ihre Antwort und überprüfen Sie diese sprachlich und strukturell (Grammatik, Rechtschreibung, Ausdruck, Aufbau, Überleitungen).

Stichpunktlösung zu Aufgabe 2

Introduction:
- both the USA and Canada are typical immigration countries/have a long tradition of immigration/are built on immigration
- main difference: different approaches to multiculturalism

Body:
- **a)** Canada's main goal: to find a solution
  - integrated immigration sees benefit of newcomers to society/economy (examples: steady increase, high number of immigrants having become Canadian citizens)
  - introduction of a multiculturalism-based integration policy in 1971, Charter of Rights and Freedoms in 1982, extended in 1988: Multiculturalism Act (ll. 26–30)
  - promotion of multiculturalism, "providing a sense of inclusion", support by government and communities (host of integration programs) to include newcomers into the country as "full citizens" (ll. 40–44)
  - serious discussions nationwide about how to accommodate diversity include citizens in the process
  - discussions have same status as other national discussions (for example sports, health care)
  - main reason why Canadians regard multiculturalism as an important feature of their nation
  - reason why change in demographics has happened more peacefully
- **b)** USA: treat multiculturalism as a problem
  - US concept of "melting pot"/assimilation aiming to merge different cultures in order to create a new one did not work → replaced by "salad bowl", this concept is only slightly better, as it describes cultures living independently/unconnectedly side by side
  - stop to unlimited immigration at the beginning of 20th century: immigration seen as a problem not as a benefit/contribution to society
  - since 1971 no new legislation regarding immigration integration or multiculturalism has been introduced, number of immigrants applying for full citizenship is rather small compared to Canada
  - lack of integration, ghettoization in large cities (NY, Detroit, LA, San Francisco), see films *8 Mile, Gran Torino,* novels *The Joy Luck Club, Tortilla Curtain:* illustrate the distance between white Americans and other cultures; migrants voluntarily form their own small communities due to lack of integration
  - for mutual understanding it is necessary that different cultures get to know each other, accept/tolerate diversity (example: text)
  - financial/economic/moral/political support necessary for integration, motivation/goal for newcomers to support the new country (example: *Gran Torino:* white protagonist helps Asian neighbours to feel safe)
  - integration at local/community/regional and governmental level necessary

Conclusion:
- immigration: process connected with globalization, in the "global village" the main goal is to live together for the sake of the community; opportunities for and contribution of newcomers should be welcomed for the support of the community
- exclusion might lead to racial tensions/riots (example: riots in the north of Paris, France) which could mean the end or the destruction of a community

3 "Is wanting to preserve ...?" Discuss.

> **HINWEIS** Diese Aufgabe gehört zum Anforderungsbereich III. Ihre Aufgabe ist es, die im Zitat aufgeworfene Frage zu diskutieren (Operator *discuss*). Das bedeutet, dass Sie die Pro- und Kontra-Seite dieser Frage beleuchten und anschließend aus der Argumentation eine fundierte Schlussfolgerung ziehen sollen, die auch Ihren begründeten Standpunkt enthält.

Lösungsschritte zu Aufgabe 3

1	Lesen Sie den Text und unterstreichen Sie für die Diskussion notwendige Textstellen.

2	Sammeln Sie Material für den zu erstellenden Text (z. B. in Form einer Mindmap) und strukturieren Sie dieses sinnvoll:
	■ Einleitung: Bezug zum vorgegebenen Text
	■ Hauptteil:
	  a) vorgegebene Frage erläutern
	  b) Pro-Argumente
	  c) Kontra-Argumente
	■ Schlussteil: Abwägen der Argumente/eigene Meinung/Rückbezug auf vorgegebenes Problem

3	Formulieren Sie Ihre Antwort und überprüfen Sie diese sprachlich (Grammatik, Rechtschreibung, Ausdruck) und strukturell (Paragrafen, Argumente, Überleitungen).

Stichpunktlösung zu Aufgabe 3

Introduction:
- immigration means people of different cultural heritage live together; immigrants often seen as intruders in already existing culture
- discussion of "Leitkultur" in Germany a couple of years ago mirrors the problem implied in the question, i.e. the wish to preserve one's own cultural identity and the fears that one's own culture could get lost in a multicultural society

Body:
- **a)** problem raised: preservation of one's cultural heritage often seen negatively, sometimes associated with racism
- **b)** desire to preserve one's own culture often has a negative connotation, has been used to justify cultural dominance (examples: Ku Klux Klan, Nazis)
  - globalization/migration: permanent encounter of different cultures, chance to enrich one's own culture (examples: calmness of Buddhism contrasts the hectic Western lifestyle, different kinds of food, music styles)
  - chance to question the values/ethics of one's own culture
  - due to various influences (example: language) from different cultures, a "pure" culture is no longer possible → "global" culture
- **c)** but: people also rely on language, traditions, customs, music, religion, history being passed on to descendants
  - cultural identity defines one's own sense of belonging, one's roots, it provides self-confidence and the sense of uniqueness of a community/culture that has to be passed on in the future
  - culture expresses inner self of people, people gain strength from it
  - to preserve one's own culture is a human instinct, it means to preserve oneself/one's individuality
  - diversity of unique cultures is necessary to survive globally as it defines individuality
  - possible result might be global cultureless people with no identity, who might easily be abused or manipulated

Conclusion:
- preservation of individual cultures is necessary as the global history of a diverse humankind is to be preserved and passed on
- danger: racial/cultural fanaticism leads to exclusion, social tensions, complete failure in society, as observed in countries like France or Germany (see text)
- text also provides a positive example of how to live diversity

Vorschlag C ■ LÖSUNGSVORSCHLAG 2012

> **NÜTZLICHE WENDUNGEN Kontraste ausdrücken / expressing contrasts**
> - On the one hand ..., on the other hand ...
> - In contrast to ...
> - In comparison with ... / when compared with ...
> - Neither ... nor ...
> - In spite of / despite ...
> - Although / though ...
> - However, ...
> - Whereas / while ...

Vorschlag C: Environment/Attitudes towards Work

Teil A: Aufgabe zur Sprachmittlung
A group of environmental ... Summarize the excerpt ...

> **HINWEIS** Diese Aufgabe verlangt verschiedene Fähigkeiten. Sie sollen entsprechend der Aufgabe Informationen zusammenfassen und diese sinngemäß und mit eigenen Worten in die Fremdsprache übertragen. Es wird keine reine Übersetzung verlangt. Lösen Sie sich unbedingt von der Sprache und dem Stil der deutschen Textvorlage. Beachten Sie, für wen und für welchen Anlass der Text zusammengefasst werden soll (siehe Aufgabenstellung), denn dies bestimmt das zu verwendende Sprachregister.

Lösungsschritte zur Sprachmittlung

1	Lesen Sie den Text in Material A, markieren Sie die für die Aufgabe relevanten Informationen und fassen Sie sie zusammen.
2	Übertragen Sie die Informationen sinngemäß ins Englische (keine Übersetzung vom Deutschen ins Englische vornehmen, aber Fachbegriffe beachten).
3	Formulieren Sie den Text aus, achten Sie dabei auf den Textzusammenhang und den Adressaten, überarbeiten Sie Ihren Text sprachlich kritisch.

Ausführlicher Lösungsvorschlag zur Sprachmittlung

The online newspaper article "Öl – war da was?" published in *Die Zeit*, July 22, 2010 (www.zeit.de), provides the author's personal view on the oil-spill disaster in the Gulf of Mexico and on US environmental policy.

First, the author refers to another environmental catastrophe to which citizens reacted strongly, after which Congress and President Nixon passed several laws to protect the environment. This catastrophe in 1970 was a major impetus for the beginning of the environmental movement in the USA.

These reactions are shown in sharp contrast to the oil-spill disaster in Florida: here the US government seemed helpless. Usually, an environmental disaster stimulates a learning process for the population and an appropriate reaction by the government: this has not happened in this case. The temporary halt to deep-sea drilling has been cancelled by the US judiciary, and President Obama's calls for a new energy policy are not regarded as important. People seem to have got used to environmental disasters because they occur so often and the government does not react to those disasters any longer. This phenomenon is not only observed in the USA but also in many other parts of the world.

Finally, the author claims that there may be another debate about climate protection but does not know of any person or government who would be interested in sparking such a debate, as most are predominantly concerned with their re-election and the opinion of voters.

(237 words)

2012 LÖSUNGSVORSCHLAG ■ Vorschlag C

Teil B: Verkürzte Textaufgabe

1 Describe the situation.

> **HINWEIS** Diese Aufgabe gehört zu den Anforderungsbereichen I und II. Sie sollen in dieser Aufgabe nur <u>einen</u> Aspekt des Textes, die im Text dargestellte Situation, beschreiben (Operator: *describe*). Schreiben Sie einen Einleitungssatz, lösen Sie sich sprachlich von der Textvorlage und verwenden Sie die Präsenszeitformen.

Lösungsschritte zu Aufgabe 1

1	Lesen Sie den Text in Material B und markieren Sie nur wesentliche Informationen, die sich auf die Situation beziehen.
2	Entwerfen Sie Ihren Text: ■ Einleitung: Autor, Textsorte, Titel, Quelle, Situation ■ Hauptteil: Schlüsselinformationen über die im Text dargestellte Situation der Protagonistin
3	Formulieren Sie Ihren Text aus. Übernehmen Sie keine Textzitate und kommentieren Sie nichts.

Ausführlicher Lösungsvorschlag zu Aufgabe 1

This extract from Moyez G. Vassanji's novel *No New Land,* published in Toronto in 1991, describes the situation Fatima finds herself in before and after she has read a letter from university.

When her mother calls her at work about the letter from university, Fatima immediately rushes home to read it, hoping for good news. When going up in the lift she is polite but looks down on the people returning home from work. She is excited because she is aware of the letter's importance for her future life and even starts praying although she has never believed in doing so. In this way she unwillingly copies her mother's behaviour although she despises it. Having hurried to her apartment she grabs the letter from her mother, tears it open, reads it and falls down on the sofa in disappointment. The good news she has been hoping for has not materialized although she has received good grades at school. Her hopes turn into anger and grief as she cannot study pharmacy, which she has wanted to do, and has to put up with Arts and Science – something she regards as impractical. Her dream of becoming rich seems to have vanished with this decision. Her mother, on the other hand, cannot understand her daughter's disappointment: for her any kind of education is a path to success.

(224 words)

2 Compare Fatima's attitude to that of immigrants …

> **HINWEIS** Diese Aufgabe gehört zu den Anforderungsbereichen II und III. Sie sollen die Haltung der Protagonistin mit der von Einwanderern in die USA vergleichen (Operator: *compare*) und dafür auf Hintergrundwissen aus dem Unterricht zurückgreifen. Dazu müssen Sie Gemeinsamkeiten und Unterschiede benennen und eine angemessen fundierte Schlussfolgerung ziehen.

Lösungsschritte zu Aufgabe 2

1	Lesen Sie den Text und markieren Sie für den Vergleich notwendige Textstellen, suchen Sie sich einen angemessenen Bezug für Ihren Vergleich, notieren Sie Gemeinsamkeiten und Unterschiede.

2	Strukturieren Sie Ihren Text:
	■ Einleitung: Aspekte des *American Dream*
	■ Hauptteil:
	  a) Fatimas Haltung
	  b) Haltung von Immigranten, Gemeinsamkeiten und Unterschiede
	■ Schlussteil: Bewertung, Bezug zu anderen Ländern

3	Formulieren Sie den Text aus, achten Sie auf Überleitungen zwischen den einzelnen Textabschnitten und überprüfen Sie Ihren Text kritisch hinsichtlich Rechtschreibung, Grammatik und Ausdruck.

Stichpunktlösung zu Aufgabe 2

Introduction:
- immigrants settled in the USA/Canada with high hopes for a new life as expressed by the American Dream, like political or religious freedom or financial success

Body:
- **a)** Fatima: representative of the second generation of immigrants
  - not satisfied with her parents' achievements, ambitious girl, gets good marks at school
  - eager to leave the apartment block that identifies her as an immigrant/outsider
  - does not care about her parents' religion, behaves arrogantly to those in her parents' generation, forgetting that they have laid the foundation for her to receive a proper education
  - tries to be different from the other immigrants, feels a sense of belonging with successful people
  - wants to study pharmacy not only to become rich but to study something "feminine", "tangible" with more "scope" (ll. 25-27) – something sophisticated that would lead to earning a lot of money and not being a poor immigrant any longer
  - extremely disappointed as her dreams are destroyed – nightmarish situation
- **b)** Fatima's parents belong to the first generation of immigrants: they worked hard to start a new life, took any job they were offered to provide a good education for their children
  - their dream was fulfilled, they are satisfied with Fatima's results as "any education was a way out, a way up" (l. 30)
  - similarities between both groups are: ambition and the will to work hard for their success/earn enough money ("become rich", l. 22), their belief in the American Dream
  - difference is that nowadays there are different immigration groups – legal and illegal ones
  - illegal immigrants do not get fair treatment/equal opportunities, have no access to education/health care (example T. C. Boyle's *Tortilla Curtain*), often face racial harassment
  - despite working hard they have no chance to improve their life, the American Dream often turns into a nightmare (example: the film *8 Mile*)
  - they turn to other sources of income: drug dealing, human trafficking, theft

Conclusion:
- attitudes have not greatly changed from generation to generation, although today immigrants have to face different economic conditions such as the financial crisis, which makes it more difficult to earn a living
- descendants of immigrants are not satisfied with just any improvement in their situation but want to <u>choose</u> how they move up
- new group of immigrants who do not want to work hard but only to "become rich", sometimes turning to crime as their source of income

3 Discuss how important money is for you when choosing ...

> **HINWEIS** Diese Aufgabe gehört zum Anforderungsbereich III. In dieser Aufgabe sollen Sie abwägen, welche Rolle Geld bei der Berufsfindung für Sie spielt (Operator: *discuss*). Auch bei einer persönlichen Relevanz der Aufgabe benötigen Sie objektive und gut begründete Pro- und Kontra-Argumente, die Sie gegeneinander abwägen, damit Sie zu einer fundierten Schlussfolgerung gelangen können. Der vorliegende Text muss als Ausgangspunkt benutzt werden. Eine strukturierte Vorarbeit bewahrt Sie davor, sich nur einseitig auf den eigenen Erfahrungsbereich zu beziehen.

Lösungsschritte zu Aufgabe 3

1	Lesen Sie den Text und markieren Sie wichtige Punkte, auf die Sie sich in Ihrer Argumentation beziehen wollen. Sammeln Sie weitere Pro- und Kontra-Argumente und belegen Sie diese mit Beispielen.

2	Strukturieren Sie Ihren Text:
	■ Einleitung: Bedeutung von Geld, Bezug zum Text
	■ Hauptteil:
	a) Geld ist ein wichtiger Faktor
	b) Geld ist kein wichtiger Faktor
	■ Schlussteil: eigene Meinung/Ausblick auf die Zukunft
3	Formulieren Sie Ihren Text aus, achten Sie auf Überleitungen zwischen den einzelnen Abschnitten und überprüfen Sie Ihren Text sprachlich (Grammatik, Rechtschreibung, Ausdruck).

Stichpunktlösung zu Aufgabe 3

Introduction:
- "Money makes the world go around": money seems to play an overwhelming role within Western societies as advertisements lure people from one shopping experience to the next; the costs of living and of supporting a family are constantly rising; "becoming rich" seems to be the solution to these problems for many people
- it also is Fatima's answer when asked about her future, her chance to get away from her present immigrant status
- money is the clear distinction between immigrant children like Fatima and other children who want to study something sophisticated for its own sake, not for the money

Main body:
- **a)** when choosing a job, money is a motivating factor as you can:
  - provide a good lifestyle for yourself and your family
  - choose where to live, unlike the family in the novel, which has to live in a high-rise building due to their low income
  - enjoy more expensive free-time activities such as sailing, riding, playing polo, getting to know other influential people and so create a social network that might help you further your career
  - offer your children a wider range of extracurricular activities (learning to play an instrument, studying another language), thus providing them with a good foundation for their futures and supporting their talents to give them advantages
  - enjoy cultural activities like theatre/opera performances and thus broaden your intellectual horizons
- **b)** money is not a motivating factor as one should choose a job that best suits one's abilities and qualifications
  - when choosing a career, people often want it to provide self-fulfillment, inspiration, and innovation
  - being successful also means you can help, change, or develop parts of society
  - examples: organizations for people who voluntarily help the homeless or poor people, like "Die Arche" or "Die Tafel"; members dedicate some of their time and abilities to society for the benefit of people in need
  - people who do research to fight deadly diseases often work overtime without pay to find a solution
  - doctors in emergency rooms do more than they are paid for when saving people

Conclusion:
- the reasons mentioned in part b) are more valuable because they have less interest in the well-being of the individual than in the well-being of many/of society
- however, the importance of money in a financially-oriented world cannot be denied
- one's priority should not be money when choosing a job